View of Camel's Hump from the Dean Trail

Fifty Hikes in Vermont

Walks, Day Hikes
and Backpacking Trips in
the Green Mountain
State

Ruth and Paul Sadlier

Updated by
Betsy Bates and
Gerald C. Slager

New Hampshire
Publishing Company
Somersworth

Thank you, John

International Standard Book Number: 0-89725-013-3
Library of Congress Catalog Card Number: 79-92572

First edition published in 1974. Second edition published in 1981.

Published by New Hampshire Publishing Company
Somersworth, New Hampshire 03878
Printed in the United States of America

Photographs on pages 15, 100, and 159 courtesy of the Vermont Development Agency; photograph on page 113 courtesy of Jay Peak, Inc. All other photographs by the authors.

Assistance with the second edition from members of the Green Mountain Club; John W. Cioffredi of the Rutland Recreation Department; Thomas H. Hubbard of the South Burlington Recreation Department; Louis Webster, Ellen Goodell, and Paul Schaberg of Burlington; and Mrs. John McDill of Woodstock is gratefully acknowledged.

Design by Wladislaw Finne

Note to the Revised Edition

This second edition of *Fifty Hikes in Vermont* has been completely revised, updated, and redesigned. All of the original fifty routes were rehiked by two experienced Vermont hikers, Betsy Bates and Gerald C. Slager. They recorded the changes that had occurred on those hikes in the years since the guide was first published in 1974: changes in driving directions, parking instructions, trailhead locations, prominent manmade landmarks, and trail routings. They also noted any significant changes in the forest cover. All these comments were incorporated in the revised text. Additional information was obtained in some cases from the groups or organizations responsible for maintaining individual trails. Two trails that appeared in the original edition have been dropped because they are no longer open to the public, and two new hiking areas have been added.

This edition includes completely new maps. The United States Geological Survey topographical sheets have been used as the base maps to depict the route of each hike. These new maps are more accurate and, because they show surrounding terrain and landmarks, are more useful in figuring out where you are and what you are looking at.

Future changes in roads, trailheads, property ownership, and the trails themselves will, of course, affect the descriptions in this edition. If you do find the hikes changed from their descriptions here, please let the author and publisher know so that corrections may be made in a future edition. Address comments and suggestions to: Editor, *Fifty Hikes*, New Hampshire Publishing Company, Box 70, Somersworth, NH 03878.

Somersworth, NH
March 1981

Contents

Introduction

Introductory Hikes

Southern Vermont

Central Vermont

Northern Vermont

Backpacking Hikes

With increasing amounts of leisure time, people are turning more to healthy outdoor activities. Hiking and backpacking offer myriad opportunities to gain relief from the complexities and luxuries of our modern world. What we might term the "appeal of the wilds" draws us out into the clean, invigorating air of scenic woodlands and towering mountains. And yet, there is more to hiking than just walking along a trail or looking at a view. We gain appreciation for nature's unique values: simplicity, silence, and solitude. We learn that we must depend more upon ourselves than on external aids. We learn that by "roughing it" we can better appreciate what we have. In the end, we learn more about ourselves.

The Fifty Hikes

We have selected these fifty hikes from all sections of Vermont. Some trips are clearly for experienced hikers only and some are designed for the inexperienced and groups with young children, but the majority will reward any reasonably fit hiker or hiker-to-be. This selection includes trips on Vermont's five highest peaks (all over 4,000 feet) and twenty different excursions of the well-known and well-used Long Trail. The other thirty hikes, however, follow the theme of (Vermont Poet Laureate) Robert Frost's poem "The Road Not Taken." They introduce you to some of the less traveled peaks and areas.

Forty-five of the hikes are day trips. Of these, eight are introductory hikes. The remaining five offer chances for extended backpacking journeys. Two can be handled on a normal weekend (two days/one night); two, on a long weekend (three days/two nights); and one, in a week (five days/four nights). In addition, Hikes 47 and 49 can be combined to form a second five-day/four-night outing.

In the seven years between publica-tion of the first edition of this guide and the completely revised edition you are now reading, many of the fifty hikes have undergone changes. Some of these alterations in trails or terrain are insignificant, while others are not. Two of the original fifty hikes had to be dropped from this edition. Both had crossed private land to which the public had been granted access. In one case, the owner asked that the trail be deleted because the property had been subjected to undue stress and abuse from hikers, and in the other, the land had changed hands and the current owner had other plans for the property's use. The Mount Tom and Red Rocks Park hikes, both on public land, are new to this edition. In all other cases, changes that had occurred in the years between editions were incorporated into the text of the appropriate hike.

Distance, Hiking Time, Vertical Rise, and Class

These categories appear at the beginning of each hike and give you a summary of what lies ahead. They should help you decide if a particular hike matches your abilities and the time you have available.

Distance gives the mileage, to the nearest tenth, from a hike's start to its finish. Almost all the hikes return you to your starting point, either via a loop or by the same trail. Three of the overnights, Hikes 47, 48, and 49, are exceptions; on these you start at one point and finish miles away, necessitating additional transportation arrangements.

Don't be surprised to find some mileage differences between those listed in this book and the same ones appearing on trail signs erected by the Green Mountain Club and the U.S. Forest Service. For example, we measured the East Branch Trail to Somerset Reservoir at 4.7 miles one way, but read on the Forest Service sign that it was 6.5 miles and in the Green Mountain Club's literature that it was 5.5 miles! We will not try to argue that our distances are the only true ones, although we do believe they are accurate.

We will, however, state that our *hiking times* were computed with care. We suggest you depend upon them whenever a difference in mileage occurs. Remember that the hiking time means just that; it does not include rest, lunch, or observation stops. After a couple of hikes you should know how your pace compares with our steady-but-leisurely one and be able to apply this knowledge to other hikes.

Vertical rise indicates the total amount of *upward* climbing entailed in a hike. Sometimes you will climb up and down valleys before ascending to a summit. Those preliminary upward climbs are included in the vertical rise figure. As a general rule, you can expect that the greater the vertical rise per mile, the more strenuous the hike.

In order to help you determine which hikes are appropriate for you, we have rated each by *class*. The criteria for the classifications are as follows:

Class I: Mostly flat-to-gradual grade; no obstacles.

Class II: Mostly gradual-to-moderate grade with possible isolated steep sections; little, if any, ledge climbing.

Class III: Gradual to mostly moderate grade with occasional steep sections; minimal ledge climbing, possibly requiring use of hands.

Class IV: Moderate-to-steep grade; much ledge climbing; use of hands necessary.

Class V: Mostly steep grade; extensive ledge climbing; much use of hands necessary.

Most people should not be fearful of attempting the hikes in Classes I or II, or even many of those in Class III. If time is not a factor and you can "go at your own pace" (which we recommend), you should find all of these within your reach. A few of the hikes in Class III and all those in Classes IV and V are quite strenuous. These should not be attempted by anyone who does not exercise regularly (active, sinewy youth may be the exception here). Remember that once you are on the trail and beyond the limits of civilization, you must depend upon your feet, legs, back, hands, and cardio-vascular system. Don't attempt more than you can reasonably handle.

Maps

The maps in this edition of the guidebook are based on the United States Geological Survey topographical maps. The hike routes and any important landmarks have been superimposed on the appropriate USGS map or maps for the area. In many cases the maps provided here will be sufficient, but if you are planning to take one of the longer hikes, it would be wise to obtain a separate USGS map to carry with you also. The USGS maps can help orient you should you become lost, and they cover a sufficiently large area so that you identify more distant peaks when you have clear mountain views. The USGS maps are usually available at sporting goods stores. They can also be obtained, along with an index to the state of Vermont, directly from the government. Write to: United States Geological Survey, 1200 South Eads Street, Arlington, Virginia 22202.

Vermont and the Green Mountains

While touring the lake that now bears his name, on July 4, 1609, Samuel Champlain made the first recorded mention of the Green Mountains. Of all the mountains in the world, they are among the oldest (close to 400 million years old). They once rivaled the heights of such young peaks as Mount McKinley and Mount Rainier.

The bedrock that makes up most of the Green Mountain range was formed beneath the ocean, eons ago, of sea shells, shale, sand, and sedimentary clay. The hot, molten interior of the earth caused great upheavals in the ocean floor, pushing the sea back and giving birth to the mountains—which reared their heads to cool slowly. Fragmentation and additional eruptions in the earth's surface gave rise to other new peaks.

The Ice Age brought glaciers. Organic life was crushed beneath frozen mile-thick masses. During Ice Age "summers," rivers coursed across the face of glaciers and ferried quantities of rocks to southern New England and Long Island Sound. Farmers have been plowing these glacial deposits out of fields and piling them into stone walls for hundreds of years.

The Green Mountains were molded and carved by the thousands of years of glacial advancement and recession. Vermont's mountains today have approximately the same elevation and contours as they did at the time of the final recession of the glaciers.

When only the Indians inhabited America, Vermont was a virtual wilderness. Early settlers appeared and began to cut trees to clear land for cattle, corn, towns, and industries. They also reduced vast numbers of trees to cinders to obtain potash, which was in high demand for English industries. Logging empires of the 1800s ruthlessly slaughtered the virgin forests and exported the lumber to build new towns and cities along the Atlantic coast.

There were continual murmurings from conservationists about the large-scale pillaging of woodlands. In 1891

Joseph Battell confronted the Vermont legislature and pleaded for protection of the wildlands. This "forestry movement" led to the founding of the Forest Association.

In 1912 the duties of this association were extended. State-owned model forests demonstrated the advantages of scientific cutting and planting to private woodlot owners. Forest management for both conservation and commerce came under this single authority. Lumbermen realized that it was good business to replace trees and perhaps increase their numbers, for future harvests.

Other groups have also played roles in preserving some of Vermont's forest lands. Many people were introduced to the Green Mountains at the "Summit Houses." By the 1850s paths had been trodden to most of the highest peaks in Vermont. To accommodate the lucrative city tourist trade, carriage roads were built up most of them. Equinox Mountain, Mount Ascutney, Camel's Hump, Mount Mansfield, Lincoln Mountain, and Snake Mountain all offered bed and board in their summit houses. Sunsets, sunrises, hiking, dancing, and entertainment occupied the guests. Most of the summit houses were eventually lost to declines in business, fires,. . .or porcupines.

The Green Mountain Club has also been instrumental in fostering trail growth and care in Vermont, chiefly along the famous Long Trail, which runs 262 miles from the Massachusetts border in the south to the Canadian border in the north. The club was formed in 1910 and now has active chapters throughout the state and outside. The GMC sponsors caretakers at the huts along the Long Trail, maintains the shelters and the trails, contributes to the ranger-naturalist programs on Camel's Hump and Mount Mansfield, and is responsible for the Long Trail Patrol trail crew. The organization is a tremendous resource for hikers; information about the Green Mountain Club, its activities, and its publications, can be obtained from its professionally staffed headquarters by writing to: Green Mountain Club, 43 State Street, Montpelier, Vermont 05602.

Seasonal Hiking

The Vermont hiking season is limited only by your preference and ability. Fall and winter are our favorite times to go. When the leaves start to turn, you are treated to one of nature's wonders. Cool air and rainbow colors combine to give you a "natural high." Few regions of the world possess the large tracts of broadleaved trees and favorable weather conditions that produce the vivid fall colors we enjoy in Vermont. As the air gets crisper and leaves tumble, light snow blankets the trails. Not deep enough to be a hindrance, this covering is dotted with animal tracks that unfold like a story book as you walk along. Heavy snows mean it's time to break out the snowshoes. (We don't suggest that novices begin their hiking in winter.)

Spring brings sprouting greens and lingering reminders of winter. Remember that snow may remain at higher elevations into May. Trails may be cluttered by trees and branches and be rutted in spots. June and July offer plenty of sunny days—and bugs. Take along plenty of insect repellent. If you like the feel of sweat dropping off your brow and dampening the small of your back, July and August are the months for you. September sees the end of bugs, but the days are still warm and the skies are often crystal clear.

Rules and Regulations

You do not leave these behind when departing from civilization. Most rules and regulations have been developed to help us preserve woodlands and the wildlife living therein. Philosophies such as "leave nothing but footprints" carry important messages, but they are not specific enough to check the careless rush of mankind.

Fire represents the greatest danger to our forests. The state of Vermont, accordingly, has laid down careful rules. Portable burners are classified as open fires from April 1 to November 1, and a campfire permit is required for all fires outside developed areas, regardless of the type of fuel used. Local fire wardens or district forest rangers can supply these permits. Fires may be built in authorized fireplaces on state land and at shelters within the Green Mountain National Forest. Building fires on private property without the owner's consent is prohibited by state law from April 1 to November 1 (existence of a shelter, though, indicates that consent has been given for use of the stove or fireplace therein.)

Fees are collected for use of state park facilities and Long Trail lodges. Large groups should carry tents when planning to stay overnight at a lodge or shelter in order to prevent the overcrowding their sizable numbers might cause.

Hikers who take dogs along with them should note that Vermont's state parks have leash laws. If in doubt, check ahead of your planned visit.

For additional information about hiking on Federal lands, contact: Forest Supervisor, Green Mountain National Forest, Rutland, Vermont 05701. Further information about hiking on state forest lands or in state parks can be obtained from: Department of Forest, Parks, and Recreation, Agency of Environmental Conservation, Montpelier, Vermont 05602.

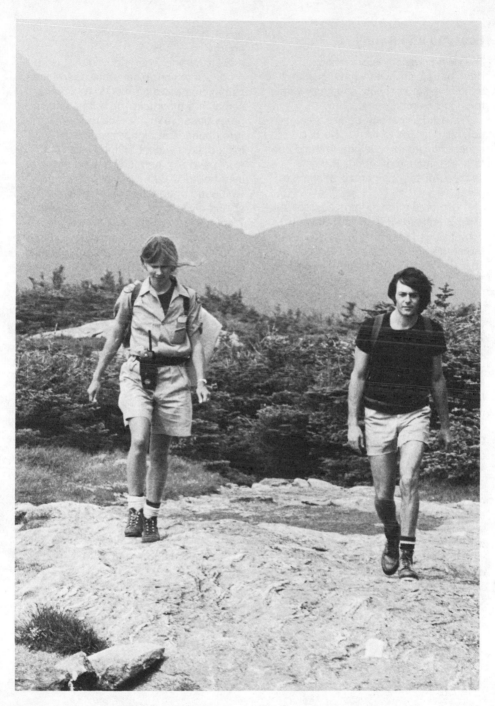

Rangers patrolling Mount Mansfield

First Aid and Safety

The best medicine is prevention. Become familiar with what lies ahead, bring suitable supplies, and know what to do in an emergency.

Traveling alone can be the greatest potential danger to hikers. *Do not underestimate this danger.* With no one to assist in case of accident the chances of serious complications are great.

Brush up on first-aid procedures and bring a first-aid kit with you. Have a compass and map and know how to use them. In Vermont the compass points about 15 degrees west of true north. Take a flashlight and extra batteries, just in case. If you do become lost or injured, don't panic. Remain calm, assess your situation, and act according to your knowledge of the area.

Whether you plan a day hike or a backpacking trip, you should carry some foodstuffs beyond what you expect to consume, at least enough for one extra meal. For an energy treat, you might consider cheese rather than chocolate. Cheeses have a high energy output; the drier ones, such as Romano, Parmesan, Provolone, and Kasseri, are the best. Even relatively dry Swiss and Cheddar have a high water content, so weigh more. Most people do not realize that because of its high fat content (more than fifty percent in unsweetened varieties), chocolate is much harder to digest than other candy. Eating large amounts of it just before or during strenuous activity often produces an upset stomach, instead of a spurt of energy.

Be sure you wear clothing that is appropriate to your planned hike, and then pack some extra garments. If you are climbing a mountain you will need long pants because of unpredictable temperature changes at higher elevations. Wide-legged, light-weight rainpants are both warm and dry, and they pull on easily over boots. Cotton chamois shirts provide good button-over warmth. You should always carry a woolen sweater. Wool, even if it gets wet, will keep you warm. And the hooded parka of a rainsuit can serve as either wetgear or windbreaker. We bring along featherweight rainsuits on even the sunniest of days.

Preserving Our Heritage

Finally, here are some guidelines for insuring that what we enjoy today will be there for others to enjoy tomorrow:

Keep your group small.
Stay only a short time in one place.
Leave campsites cleaner than you found them.
Carry out empty what you carried in full.
Pick up the litter of less thoughtful persons.
Don't contaminate water.
Bury body waste.
Burn burnables only if a fire is permitted.
Do not cut trees or branches.
Leave no sign of your presence.

1

Texas Falls Nature Trail

Class: I
Distance (round trip): 1 mile
Hiking time: 3/4 hour
USGS 7.5' Bread Loaf

The 240,000-acre Green Mountain National Forest offers a wide variety of natural attractions. This showcase of preserved land stretches nearly two-thirds the length of Vermont. A trip through the forest is not just a hike in the woods but rather an excursion into Vermont itself. Rolling countryside, small towns, and slackening pace typify the simpler, quieter way of life that is Vermont.

A leisurely walk through the Texas Falls Recreation Area, on the eastern edge of the Green Mountain National Forest near Hancock, will introduce you to the state's natural endowments. Here the Hancock Branch of the White River pours its waters through an awesome descending gorge in a unique display of nature's magnitude. Explanatory guideposts along the nature trail help you better understand the forest's ways and the need for its careful management in today's technological world.

On the Robert Frost Memorial Drive (VT 125), go east 12.9 miles from Middlebury or west 3 miles from Hancock. Turn north onto the road for the Texas Falls National Forest Recreation Area. After .5 mile you will reach a parking area on the left and a sign for the Texas Falls observation site on the right.

A path leads from the road down some stone steps to an attractive setting. A combination wood and stone fence guides you along the trail. You see below a deep gorge with water rushing through. Flowing from a flat pool up to the left, it gushes down into a white, frothy basin. Then slithering over a smooth ledge, it winds and spills its way to quieter pools below. Towering hemlocks help focus your view upon the surging water.

Wind your way up more manmade stone steps to the signed intersection. A right turn leads you along a spur trail and an overlook below the gorge. The sound of pounding water fills your ears as you look the length of the gorge and see several waterfalls, one atop the other.

Return to the intersection and begin the interpretive section of the trail. Almost immediately you come to post #1. The dying and decaying trees of the forest help to enrich the soil around them with new organic material. Leaves and other natural materials fall to the ground and decay, adding more vital nutrients to the soil. At this station you will observe logs undergoing the process of decay.

Opposite post #1 is another spur to an overlook. Log benches offer a chance to just sit and linger in this peaceful setting. From here you can see the upper section of the falls.

The flat, spongy trail leads on to post #2. The source of the Hancock Branch is a forested watershed. Because of the overhanging branches and foliage of the trees and the carpet of leaves on the forest floor protecting the soil from rain erosion, the stream remains unmuddied.

Passing a log bench, the trail reaches posts #3 and #4. Behind post #3 are low plants known as witch hobble. They are a favorite food of deer. Look closely to see if any of their tops have been nibbled.

Post #4 marks the location of a massive boulder. Through the process of symbiosis, a plant community thrives on top of this great rock. Its greenish-grey, crustlike growth is a type of lichen and is composed of two distinctly different plants. Water is collected by the sponge-like fungus. The alga uses this water in photosynthesis to produce food for both

Texas Falls

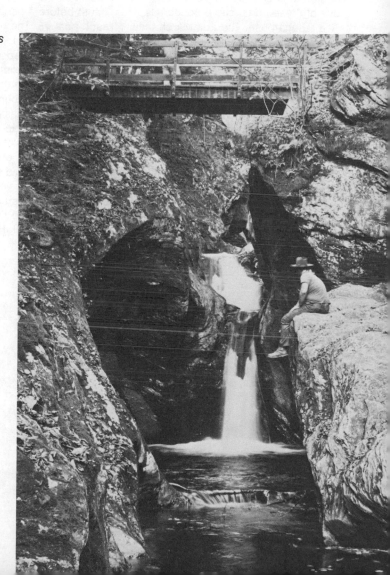

itself and the fungus. Thus, the two plants are interdependent; neither could live alone on the rock's surface.

As you begin a gradual climb, the hillside to your right rises steeply. The trail continues to parallel the river. Scattered openings in the trees enable you to glimpse the rushing stream.

Approaching post #5 you can see where the river courses beneath the road bridge. This station identifies a sugar maple. This is the tree from which the famous Vermont maple syrup comes. To be fit for tapping, a tree must be at least forty years old, about sixty feet high, and one foot in diameter. A grove of these prime sap producers is called a sugarbush. The first March thaw is the time when new tap holes are drilled. Buckets are hung on the sap spouts and checked several times a week through March and into April. It takes about forty-five gallons of boiled-down sap to produce a gallon of pure maple syrup.

The trail begins a slight descent as it approaches post #6. Here only twenty feet of a large hemlock remain standing; its top lies on the side of the trail decaying. Many smaller ones are in the area. Hemlocks may grow to eighty feet in height and three feet in diameter. They feature irregularly arranged, half-inch-long needles with twin silvery lines on the underside. Unlike balsam, hemlock needles are not fragrant when crushed. The hemlock is part of the diet of a variety of wildlife. Porcupines chew on the bark, and the seeds are eaten by squirrels and birds.

Post #7, just ahead on the left, displays a botanical oddity. Maple trees normally have a single stem and root system. The maple near the sign post has one root system supporting a number of stems. This is the result of the original stem breaking. The hardiest sprouts formed by the dormant buds at the root collar survived, forming this mass.

Just before a bend in the trail you reach post #8. The rows of small holes girdling the hemlock here were made by a yellow-bellied sapsucker. This woodpecker digs out holes and eats the inner bark. During this process sap oozes from the wound. The sapsucker returns later to feast upon any insects attracted to the sap.

After this last station, the trail drops down to the road, ending opposite a picnic area. You could simply follow the park road back to your car, but why not reverse your route and enjoy it once again? With ample time to picnic and relax, you have all the ingredients for a perfect day.

2

Merck Forest Nature Trail

Class: I
Distance (round trip): 1.5 miles
Hiking time: 1 hour
Vertical rise: 400 feet
USGS 7.5' Pawlet

The 2,600 acres of woodland, meadows, ponds, and streams that comprise the Merck Forest in Rupert were set aside by George W. Merck in 1950. He felt a close kinship to the land and believed that these fields and forests represented typical Vermont upland farms, then rapidly dying out as commercial ventures. He foresaw that rapidly increasing numbers of outdoor enthusiasts would buy up and otherwise dominate Vermont's open lands and realized the need to preserve extensive areas for public use. He also hoped that the Merck Forest could show how farms might be converted to multiple-use properties.

The Merck Forest, which is run by a private foundation, is made up of several abandoned farms. Although much of the original grazing land has become forest (through both natural seeding and planting), some of the meadows are mowed to keep a balance between forest and open land. A year-round program of logging and reforestation maintains the forest's productivity. The wildlife habitats that result provide suitable homes for a variety of animals. The forest also helps visitors become better acquainted with,

and more understanding of, their environment.

This hike can be enjoyed by the entire family. Its relatively short length allows for leisurely walking and plenty of exploration. Signboards at the fourteen stations along the trail offer detailed information about tree plantations, gardens, and wildlife habitats. You'll learn about fungi, soil and climatic conditions, control of animal populations, and forest life cycles. Signs will also introduce you to the following trees along the way: white birch, sugar maple, aspen, larch, black cherry, apple, and oak.

You reach the entrance to the Merck Forest on VT 315 by driving 3.3 miles east from the junction of VT 315 and VT 153 in Rupert, or 2.6 miles west from the junction of VT 315 and VT 30 in East Rupert. Turn south onto the Merck Forest Road, which immediately forks. Bear right and drive .5 mile to the parking area. Walk to the information area near the gate. Register (for Merck Forest rules, see Hike 17) and take advantage of the pamphlets and the colorful wooden map displayed there.

Walk through the gate and down the road for approximately .2 mile to the trail junction just below the barn that houses exhibits and other programs run by the foundation. Turn right onto the path, which will lead you to the Nature Trail sign and a box containing pamphlets describing the route.

Over its first half, the trail descends gradually and then flattens out. After coming to the first signpost, which describes how environments change, turn left and follow the edge of the meadow, keeping the trees always on your left.

Just before you reach the parking area, a small footpath wanders off to the right. This trail is marked with yellow dots on the trees and will take you across the road you walked earlier to some log steps.

Continuing, you will come to a fork immediately after passing the forest diversity station. Turn left for the Spruce Loop, which is the nicest part of the hike. The spruce trees are so thick here that their lower branches have turned brown from lack of sunlight. Stop awhile at the bench and enjoy the solitude of this dense forest.

Coming out of the loop, turn left on the main trail, which leads you down to the barn. The center of the Merck Forest education program, the barn offers exhibits that introduce you to the many plants and animals that appear in the forest. Instruction in conservation education is made available. The qualified staff works efficiently to provide this—and other—helpful information.

When you are ready to leave, return to the road; your car is just a short walk to the right.

Merck Forest Nature Trail

3

Pine Hill Park

Class: I
Distance: 1 mile, more or less
Hiking time: 1/2 hour, or more
USGS 7.5' Rutland

In 1761 Governor Benning Wentworth of New Hampshire chartered Rutland. The first grantee, John Murray of Rutland, Massachusetts, christened the new settlement. A prosperous gristmill and sawmill established in the 1770s made Rutland a flourishing frontier town within a few years.

After the Civil War, Colonel Redfield Proctor returned to Rutland and transformed its one-hundred-year-old marble business into a highly successful operation. Located in the western part of Rutland, its marble deposits were among the world's richest.

Today, Rutland is a small American city, a busy center of retail trading and industrial activity. A section of the city has been preserved for natural recreational activities. Pine Hill Park sits quietly in Rutland's northwestern corner, away from the bustle of its shopping district and factories.

To reach the park, drive west on US 4 through Rutland. Shortly after crossing the cement bridge over East Creek, Route 4 bears sharply left. Turn right here onto Pierpoint Avenue. At the end of Pierpoint, just beyond the Northwest School, continue straight onto Fairview Avenue. Turn right at the end of Fairview

onto the Oak Street extension. Pine Hill Park appears quickly on your left. Park along the edge of the road.

Pine Hill Park is set up to serve many recreational needs of the residents of Rutland. In addition to the forests, fields, and meadows through which the numerous hiking trails run, the park contains baseball playing fields, picnic tables, an ice skating area, and other recreational facilities.

The trail system is elaborate, and as of this writing (1981), the individual trails were in the process of being remarked and renamed. Most of the trails are short interconnecting loops, some leading through open woods, some through fields, and others to the large meadow adjacent to the East Creek. All are blazed with yellow, white, and blue paint spots, and all are suitable for family strolls. There is also a 3-mile-long trail from the park northwest to Rocky Pond, still inside Rutland's city boundary, and then east to the Rutland Country Club. Rutland's Recreation Department (on Court Street) has plans to revise and reissue a map and pamphlets to Pine Hill Park and can be contacted for up-to-date information.

The park is a fine place to introduce

yourself to some of Vermont's flora and fauna and to examine the relationships established in the woodland community. Notice as you walk the apple trees of abandoned farmland and how pruning of the large shade trees allow this species, as well as black cherry, thornapple, and honeysuckle, to thrive. The twigs, fruits, and seeds of these trees and shrubs provide food for animals and birds.

As you come to some of the large boulders that grace the woodland, stop to examine the colonies of mosses and lichens they support. The mosses form a furry green carpet on the boulders. Lichen are composed of two types of plants: a fungus and an alga. The spongelike fungus collects water that supplies the alga with minerals and water and keeps it from drying out. In return, the alga supplies food for both the fungus and itself through the process of photosynthesis.

Rotting stumps and fallen trees also serve as ecological textbooks. Through the process of decay, they return nutrients to the surrounding soil, which living plants and trees utilize for growth. The dead trees also provide homes and food to many different kinds of small animals and insects.

Somerset Reservoir

Class: II
Distance (round trip): 9.4 miles
Hiking time: 5 hours
Vertical rise: 475 feet
USGS 15' Wilmington

If you want a full day of hiking, try the East Branch Trail to Somerset Reservoir. The route has you crossing two different rivers (one several times), skirting beaver dams, and meandering undemandingly through a number of naturally varied areas. With the prospect of a picnic at the reservoir, this hike has all the ingredients for a very satisfying day. Do note the distance and hiking time, though. You will want to allow plenty of time for rest and observation stops and for that picnic lunch. Don't get caught short or you may be forced to complete your hike in darkness.

The East Branch Trail was originally put in by the Civilian Conservation Corps as a fire trail. Although the route has been maintained by the National Forest Service, it traverses almost its entire length land belonging to the New England Power Company (NEPCO). In the winter of 1979, the hikers' suspension bridges over the Deerfield River and the East Branch, both necessary for the crossings, washed out. Neither had been replaced as of this writing (1981), but NEPCO officials had plans to replace them soon. Hikers should check with the Harriman Reservoir station of NEPCO before starting out to see if the bridges have been rebuilt.

To reach the start of the East Branch Trail from the intersection of VT 9 and VT 100 in Wilmington, go west on Route 9 for 5.4 miles. Here turn right onto a dirt road—a few yards in you'll see a sign for "Picnic Area— NEPCO"—and drive 1.8 miles to the trailhead. Park along the widened side of the road. If you look down the path, you will see a sign for the Deerfield River.

The path drops down the embankment to the bridge crossing. Assuming the bridge is in, continue to the north bank of the Deerfield, which the trail parallels upstream a short distance. At the fork, it bears right, making its way up through a grassy open field. Evergreens mix with deciduous trees as the route leads you gently up and down to the next bridge crossing, at .4 mile. If this one is in, you can cross the East Branch of the Deerfield River with ease.

Spruce and balsam needles cushion the path as it leads down evergreen lanes. The way is flat and the walking easy. Yellow birches alternate with conifers where the woods open up. The East Branch appears down to your left as you cross the first of several small streams. Logs and walkalongs help you across these waters. A good sense of balance can be helpful.

roots are all piled together to hold back the water. Once there is sufficient water to support a lodge and winter beaver activity, the dam is completed. Note also the many gnawed tree stumps and the wet meadowland filled with dead trees. Once a beaver pond, this area is in the process of becoming a meadow; it eventually will be forest again.

Swinging away from the river, the trail passes through a concentrated area of low spruces. It continues along flat terrain and at 1.7 miles swings sharply right just before reaching the river. Walking parallel to the water, you keep below a ridge line. The trail crosses a tributary at 1.9 miles and the river itself at 2.2 miles. For the next .5 mile you crisscross the water several times, traveling parallel to it on both sides.

Leaving the river, the trail becomes rocky at times as it passes through extensive hardwood forests. Slender young trees predominate here. The ground is littered with older, decaying trees. At 3.4 miles the trail approaches a large area of former beaver activity. Hundreds of barkless, sun-bleached logs lie strewn across the land. A deserted lodge can now be reached via dry land. It provides a good close-up of a beaver home.

After beavers have created a pond, muskrats often move in to enjoy it, Mink, which love muskrat meat, are the next to arrive. Although the beavers have moved on, mink still live here. You may see their droppings on the East Branch Trail.

The trail continues flat and smooth. You cross several brooks before dipping down through a large, grassy field. Rocks and roots fill the path as it parallels the river again. Twisting and turning, the well-marked trail intersects the gravel reservoir road at 4.6 miles.

Go right, and follow the winding road .1 mile up to the reservoir. Filling the horizon at the far end of Somerset Reservoir is Stratton Mountain. Glaston-

Beaver dams come into view on the left. Take time for close inspection of the engineering involved in their construction. Sticks, branches, grass, dirt, and

Beaver lodge

bury Mountain rises to the west and, by walking to the left a bit, you can see Mount Snow to the east. The picnic area and a public boat launching site are just down the road to the right.

The picnic area is also the jumping off point for several other hikes around Somerset Reservoir; there is the old Somerset Reservoir trail, and NEPCO is in the process of cutting several new trails on both sides of the lake.

5

The Pinnacle

Class: II
Distance (round trip): 1 mile
Hiking time: 1/2 hour
Vertical rise: 280 feet
USGS 15' Claremont, NH — VT

A check of old maps indicated that the Pinnacle was formerly called Plum Hill—after the Plum family who lived nearby. Its modern name, however, is a bit misleading. It is little more than a big hill.

The Pinnacle rises alongside the winding Connecticut River in Weathersfield. The Connecticut used to be a prime source of drinking water for domesticated animals. Although cows come to mind first when we think of Vermont farm animals, sheep were the state's principal livestock in the 1830s. William Jarvis, the American consul in Lisbon, imported the first Merino (i.e., long-haired) sheep to the United States in 1811 and bred them for forty-eight years on his farm in nearby Weathersfield Bow. This brought about significant changes in the woolen industry and stimulated the growth of sheep raising in the East.

Families will find the climb up the Pinnacle a pleasant outing. A wide, gradual path leads lazily upward. With its elevation of 425 feet, the peak doesn't promise you wide, far-reaching views. But the open overlook nestled in the summit's snowy white birches directs your gaze down to the peaceful Connecticut River Valley and beyond to the rolling hills of New Hampshire.

The Pinnacle is a part of Wilgus State Park. From the junction of VT 44 and US 5 in Windsor, drive south on US 5 for 6.1 miles to the park entrance on the left. Pay your 50¢ per day, per person recreation fee and park in the designated area to the right. (The park also has tent and trailer sites.) Cross US 5 and walk to the trail's start just north of the park entrance. Dogs should be kept on a leash.

This blue-blazed trail begins gradually and quickly makes a switchback upward to the left. Paralleling the road below, you follow a wide, flat trail between stands of hardwoods. In the fall you may identify these trees by the leaves and fruit they shed on the ground. The oval, blunt-based leaves of the birches turn yellow. The coarse-toothed, egg-shaped leaves of the beech are light brown and often veined with yellow. Long, lobed leaves—usually light brown—and familiar acorns announce the presence of oaks. White pines spill five-clustered needles.

After this long, gradual stretch of walking, you start a swing to the right. The hillside drops off steeply to the left. Hemlocks appear frequently along the trail. Their shorter, irregularly arranged needles help distinguish them from the balsam fir. Tiny cones and rough bark further identify these evergreens.

Stands of slender white birches predominate as the path bears right. These tall, striking trees are accented by the soft green of intermingling white pine. At approximately .2 mile the blue blazes mark a sharp right turn onto a narrower trail. Watch carefully here: the wider trail you have been following continues straight ahead.

Birds abound. Watch for the hermit thrush—the Vermont State Bird. This songbird can adapt to a variety of habitats. It may live in swamps or dry uplands, overgrown pastures or thick woodlands. Though the hermit thrush exhibits a marked preference for coniferous forests, it will also abide in predominately deciduous ones. This brown bird's white breast is speckled with flecks of brown. Its bell-like song is especially pretty. The call is a low clucking, followed by a mewing sound. When

disturbed, it shows its displeasure by slowly raising its tail.

The path swings right to make one long, final ascent. This is the steepest section of the hike. Winding upward, the trail passes a simply constructed stone slab bench. Make your way over natural stone steps as you continue to climb. The trail traverses the slope from right to left, then turns right and heads straight for the summit.

After cresting two small slopes, you turn right. From here it is a short walk to the small clearing that is the top of the Pinnacle. A very faint blue blaze encircling a white birch marks the summit. A semi-circle of birch trees and ferns edge this open area. There is ample room to stretch out and enjoy the pastoral setting that unfolds to the east. You have a clear view of the Connecticut River and New Hampshire hills.

Although the blazed trail does continue steeply down to the Park campground, it is more pleasant to retrace your steps to the starting point.

Mount Hor

Class: II
Distance (round trip): 3.1 miles
Hiking time: 2 hours
Vertical rise: 748 feet
USGS 15' Lyndonville

The Mount Hor Trail, in Willoughby State Forest (see Hike 41), is a good one for leisurely leg stretching and relaxed enjoyment of panoramic views. The climb is gradual, making it an ideal trip for families and beginning hikers. The views from the overlooks at and near the summit of Mount Hor will appeal to everyone.

Much of the land in this forest has been logged out quite recently, so there is an absence of mature trees. Following common practice, the state of Vermont purchased the land after it was logged for a reasonable price. This wise method of procuring large tracts has made a beautifully primitive area available to the public.

The Mount Hor Trail is one of many trails in Willoughby State Forest maintained by the Trail Committee of the Westmore Association. This group provides a valuable and much needed service—asking, in return, only that hikers cooperate by not spreading litter along the trails. Why not carry a small bag with you and collect whatever rubbish you come upon?

To reach the gravel access road to Mount Hor, follow VT 5A for 5.7 miles from the junction of VT 5A and US 5 in West Burke or an equal distance from the intersection of VT 5A and VT 16 in Westmore. Watch for a sign to the Pisgah Mountain Trail opposite the access road. Turn in here and follow the gravel road through the woods for 1.8 miles. The Mount Hor parking area is on the right. After leaving your car, walk south along the road approximately 150 feet to the start of the trail, on the right.

The way begins as a rocky path that leads gradually upward through dense side growth. Blackberry bushes edge the trail. If you happen by in the late summer, their tangy sweetness is yours for the picking.

The trail rises briefly and then flattens out. Its sides are densely covered with young maples, elms, and birches, and with goldenrod. It is difficult to see beyond the edges of the trail because of the closely packed trees. Winding slowly upward to the right, the path levels out again. The trail is marked by dark blue blazes, with occasional black-arrowed white signs lending assistance. The going gets rockier as you near the top.

Would you normally cancel a hike because of inclement weather? If so, we ask you to reconsider if rain threatens to spoil your plans for this one—Mount Hor is a very walkable rainy day hike. Hiking in the rain produces a world of new experiences if you are properly attired. While it is necessary to pick your way more gingerly, the compensations are worth the effort. Rain beating on your body makes you feel more a part of the outdoor experience. There is also a grey-green softness to the woods during rain that is absent when the sun is shining brightly.

The trail begins an upward swing to the left over bare logs laid latticelike across the path. They provide firm footing across the soft black mud beneath. Although the way climbs relentlessly uphill now, it is rock-free and quite easy going.

A massive, lightning-scarred beech stands to the right. The trail climbs straight and more steeply. Notice the sassafras growing to the right. It is most easily identified by its forward-pointing three-lobed leaf. Clusters of dark blue berries ripen in September. Sassafras tea was a product of colonial times, and oil of sassafras was once used widely as a medicine. It is still used to perfume soap.

Watch for a small sign at the .5-mile mark on the right. It lets you know that you are about to start a "fern learn" and asks you to look for signs in the vicinity. Within a few feet on both sides of the trail about a dozen ferns are identified for you.

At the .7-mile mark the trail reaches a junction. White signs guide you left to the summit (West Lookout) and right to Willoughby Lookout. Follow the trail to the left .2 mile to the summit.

This winding spur route is marked by pale blue blazes. You have to step around or over many trees and stumps.

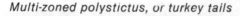

Multi-zoned polystictus, or turkey tails

Shortly the path passes over a small streamlet. Continue on this rough route as it winds upward and dips into a clearing. From here the view is to the west, encompassing ten small ponds in the valley below. They sparkle among the heavily wooded areas of Willoughby State Forest. In the distant background portions of the Green Mountains are also visible.

Return to the junction and follow the trail to Willoughby Lookout, .6 mile away. The blazes here are dark blue, and the trail is mostly flat. The way turns sharply right past a lone white birch and a small hemlock and then rises slightly. It levels out and passes a small gulch on the left. The path is soft and spongy as you pass downed trees festooned with turkey tail fungus.

The trail climbs a slight incline and then forks. Swing right and down a short embankment. A breath-taking vista—Mount Pisgah towering above the southern end of Lake Willoughby—unfolds before you. On a clear day you can catch sight of some of the White Mountains in the distance.

Return to the trail junction and follow your original route back to the access road.

7

Prospect Rock

Class: II
Distance (round trip): 1.5 miles
Hiking time: 1 hour
Vertical rise: 530 feet
USGS 15' Hyde Park

This hike curls pleasantly through cool woods, then climbs upward for the last invigorating quarter-mile to Prospect Rock. It's a satisfying trip for everyone. Experienced hikers should not omit this one because of its brevity or small vertical rise. The rock's 1,050-foot vantage point offers a prime view of the Lamoille River Valley with Sterling Range as a backdrop. You can also survey the northern slope of Mount Mansfield to the south.

Prospect Rock is on the Long Trail. To reach the access to this section of the trail drive west on VT 15 from the junction of VT 100C and VT 15 in Johnson. After 1.8 miles bear right onto the Johnson-Waterville Road. This turn is just before the Lamoille River bridge. Drive .9 mile on this road to the Ithiel Falls Camp Meeting Ground on the left. Directly across the road the Long Trail leads north up the hill and into the woods. There is very limited parking along the side of the road in front of the campground. More parking is available at an off-the-road area .2 mile east.

The Ithiel Falls Camp Meeting Ground has been in existence for over seventy-five years. Each summer the Nazarene Church sponsors a nondenominational gathering of people from across the country at this lovely location. Camping

here is available only to church members.

Follow the white blazes of the Long Trail up the incline and into the woods. A brown and white sign indicates that you are on the Long Trail North heading for Prospect Rock. Shortly after mounting the crest of this incline you cross a

View from Prospect Rock to Mount Mansfield

quick-flowing brook. Don't be surprised to see the trail cross it two more times.

This first part of the hike is along a rather broad, gradual path through the woods. Abundant greenery edges the way. Look for the hay-scented fern. Common at lower elevations, it also grows in alpine forests. It thrives in moist, partially shaded areas. The dry fronds exude the fragrant odor of hay.

Logs offer footing through occasional soft, black, muddy areas. You make your way up the narrow, gently inclined trail. Numbers of knee-high red spruce crowd the path.

The trail dips into the subdued light of an older stand of spruce. Footsteps are muffled by spruce spills over the soft earth. Sun glows softly through the thick web of branches and past the limbless reddish-brown trunks. Ahead the trail begins a sudden, steep climb through open woods. A rugged hiking stick will serve you well here. When you reach the top of this slope, bear to your right. Mushrooms and shining club moss border the trail.

Very soon you'll walk out onto Prospect Rock. Although there is no sign to mark this ledge, you will readily recognize it by the views that stretch before you.

Return via the same route.

Red Rocks Park

Class: I
Distance (around loops): 2 1/2 miles
Hiking time: 1 3/4 hours
Vertical rise: 182 feet
USGS 7.5' Burlington

If you are looking for someplace that combines peaceful woods, dramatic cliffs, outstanding lake and mountain views, and a narrow sandy beach, then make your way to Red Rocks Park. Located on the shores of Lake Champlain and Shelburne Bay, the one-hundred-acre park was purchased by the City of South Burlington in 1970 from the Hatch family, who had owned the land since 1895. Red Rocks is one of the few public accesses to Lake Champlain in Vermont. Its more than 2½ miles of interconnected trails are maintained by the South Burlington Recreation Department and are suitable for hikers and strollers of all ages. The area is also well used by cross-country skiers in winter.

To reach the park from I-89, take I-189 (exit 13) to the Shelburne-US 7 South exit, which will have you heading toward Shelburne on US 7. After only a few hundred feet, bear right onto Queen City Park Road. Stay on this road for .4 mile; after crossing a one-lane bridge, look for Central Avenue, the first road on the left. The main entrace to Red Rocks is on your right in .1 mile. The city charges a small fee from late June to early fall for parking in the main lot, but other times of the year you may simply leave your car along Central Avenue just before the main entrance drive.

To explore the park's interior first, saving the grand sweep of the panoramas along the lake cliffs for the end of your hike, start on the trails at either the northeast or northwest corner of the summer parking lot. Bearing right at major intersections, you'll wind slowly through the dense woods. On this leg you will also reach the park's highest point, 282 feet above sea level and about 100 feet higher than Lake Champlain. The view from here extends in all directions, encompassing the Green Mountains to the east, the city of Burlington to the north, and the Adirondacks to the west. Mount Mansfield is clearly visible some twenty-two miles away.

In about 1½ winding miles, you will reach the overlook at the park's western end, where Shelburne Bay meets Lake Champlain. Shelburne Point is just across the bay's mouth; the island to its right is Juniper Island. Rock Dunder is approximately midway between Shelburne Point and Juniper Island.

Now begin working your way back, staying parallel to the mile-long shoreline of Shelburne Bay. Numerous other overlooks provide equally spectacular views of the Green Mountain and the Adirondacks. There is no access to the lake from this trail, however. The cliffs drop abruptly ninety feet to the water's edge.

Most people will want to conclude their hike with a short walk from the parking lot to the narrow, 800-foot-long sandy beach at the park's southeast corner—and perhaps a swim. There are also picnic tables and rest rooms adjacent to the beach.

The Dome

Raspherrys, Blackberries

Class: III
Distance (round trip): 4.6 miles
Hiking time: 2 1/2 hours
Vertical rise: 1,648 feet
USGS 7.5' Pownal; USGS 7.5' Williamstown, MA

A tangy treat awaits you about three-quarters of the way up this trail: wild raspberries stand ready to delight your tastebuds and add a special bonus to this hike. A gradual-to-moderate climb, this hike has you scrambling over ledge as you near the Dome's summit. Once there, you'll see how this mountain got its name: a massive bulk of rounded ledge swells upward out of the surrounding terrain.

. From the junction of US 7 and VT 346 in Pownal, drive south on US 7 for 2.6 miles and turn left onto Sand Springs Road. Follow it, bearing right as the road forks, for .6 mile. Go left onto White Oaks Road. Drive 1.4 miles, past the Broad Brook Trail, past the dead-end sign, to an old road leading into the woods on the right. This is the start of the Dome Trail. Park off the road here.

Blazes for the Dome Trail are orange painted over white—resulting in a creamy color (a few of the white blazes, though, have not been painted over and some are still bright orange). The trail is well marked and easy to follow.

After leading briefly through woods, the old road becomes grassy and passes through an open field. It crosses between lines of aspen and leads through a second field. Re-entering the woods, it becomes both level and smooth. The way proceeds gradually upward. Large-toothed aspen and birches dominate the woods with their respective greenish-yellow and white trunks.

Climbing a moderate grade to the left, the road becomes rutted and rocky. Walking is easiest along the left side. You turn sharply left after cresting this grade and pass along the ridge top.

After .5 mile you come to a three-way fork. Follow the Dome Trail to the left. It makes a quick swing back to the right and continues over rocks and roots. At times the trail gouges into the earth as it struggles upward.

Another fork appears at .7 mile. Look closely and you'll see that the two paths rejoin up ahead. Follow either one. Large rocks fill the trail as it winds up through young woods. Countless thin trees swarm around occasional older, thick ones.

The Agawon Trail branches off to the right at 1 mile. Continue straight here. A sign on a big boulder marks the Dome Trail. Note the numerous oak trees throughout this area. The acorns from these trees provide food for songbirds, grouse, mourning dove, deer, bear, fox,

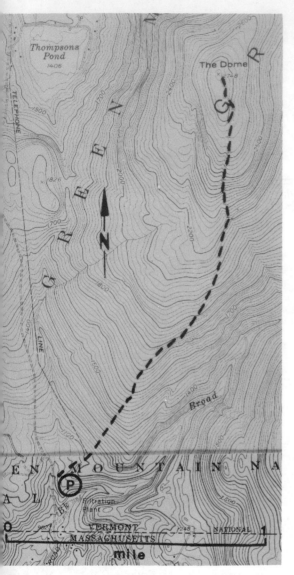

At 1.4 miles the trail intersects another old road. The remains of a junked truck mark this spot and indicate that, in the not-too-distant past, these slopes were the site of much more activity than is apparent from their present virgin appearance. Turn right and follow the road through a section of woods clogged by numerous downed trees.

Another trail branches left at 1.5 miles as you ascend a moderate slope. Rocks fill the way once again. Cresting a short, steep slope, you see masses of ledge above to the right. The path loops around behind the ledge and begins a short, steep climb. Dead beech trees support hundreds of multi-zoned polystictus. These pore fungi have thin leathery fans marked by dull-colored, concentric bands. Because of their beautiful markings, they have been nicknamed "turkey tails".

The light grey smoothness of beeches fills the woods on both sides of the trail. Various-sized rocks in the path make walking a bit adventurous. The gradual-to-moderate incline continues.

An old grassy trail branches right at 1.8 miles. Go straight ahead here. Cross several small brooks and climb along the edge of a slope as the hillside rises steeply above.

The path jogs sharply left and passes many raspberry bushes. The arching, reddish branches have prickly thorns. White flowers appear from May through July, and the red fruit ripens from June through October. There are also delicious blackberries here in early September. You'll be returning by the same route, so if you plan much berry-picking it can wait until then.

As you climb higher, the trail twists and turns through evergreens. Spruce and balsam thicken the woods from ground level to towering heights.

The path winds around and over pieces of ledge. You step up onto a

raccoon, squirrels, and chipmunks.

Scattered pines edge the trail as it climbs gradually below a ridge line. These are red pines, identifiable by their three-to-eight-inch needles in cluster of twos. The bark plates have a reddish tinge and the needles lift upward on branch ends.

The summit of the Dome

small cone of ledge surrounded by evergreens—and may think this is the top. It's not. Climb down the other side and follow the blazes up onto open ledge, amidst more spruce and balsam.

The summit lies atop a large section of smooth, humpy, white ledge lined with orange-brown streaks. Trees surround this area and block views to the north and east. The Adirondacks are to the west and Mount Greylock in Williamstown, Massachusetts, is to the south.

10

Harmon Hill

Class: II
Distance (round trip): 4.2 miles
Hiking time: 2 hours
Vertical rise: 963 feet
USGS 7.5' Bennington; USGS 7.5' Pownal; USGS 7.5' Woodford;
USGS 7.5' Stamford

It is best to do some limbering up before this particular climb. Otherwise, the steep beginning of the short hike on the Long Trail will leave you surprised and breathless. Just before the halfway point the grade slackens noticeably and remains gradual the rest of the way.

The open, grassy summit of Harmon Hill allows good views to the north and west from it southwestern-corner-of-the-state vantage point. It also invites you to spread a cloth for a picnic lunch or to stretch out on your back for cloud watching.

From the junction of VT 9 and US 7 in Bennington, drive east 3.8 miles on VT 9. Turn right immediately after crossing the highway bridge over Walloomsac Brook, and drive down into a small clearing. Park anywhere here, but don't obstruct the dirt road that continues beyond the clearing. Coming from the east, look for this turn 3.9 miles from the Prospect Mountain Ski Area. It's on the left directly before the highway bridge.

Walk from the parking area along the dirt road. White blazes and white arrows show the way. After a short distance the trail turns left off the road and leads straight up a steep embankment. After

View from Harmon Hill to Bennington; Mount Anthony beyond

cresting this slope, the path continues quite steeply up the hillside.

At .2 mile the trail joins an old road and swings sharply right. It follows this rocky road upward, sloping more gradually as it gains elevation. After 200 feet the trail leaves the road and continues up the slope to the right. Next, it swings sharply left onto still another road and then proceeds up a moderate incline bearing back to the right.

At .3 mile the route makes a switchback to the left onto another road. At the top of a rise it bears around to the right. Soon the trail narrows down to a packed dirt path. At .6 mile you cross an open swath beneath power lines. To the right you can glimpse the city of Bennington. This is a lower elevation preview of the prime views from the top of Harmon Hill.

Swinging left onto yet another old road, the trail makes a slow, rounded swing to the right. It bears left and climbs moderately along the eastern slope of an unnamed hill. Here thorny shrubs tug at your clothes.

A long stretch of muscle-straining walking marks your approach to the ridgetop above to the right. After cresting it at the 1-mile mark, you travel through a relatively flat area of open woods. The path leads between hardwoods and thick shrubs before emerging into the open.

Ravens have been spotted in this area. They are larger than the common crow, with a wing span reaching to four feet. They frequently glide in flight, wings fully extended. At home along the seacoasts as well as inland, these omnivorous birds have adopted a favorite seagull trick. They will break open shellfish by dropping them onto rocks from high above.

Meandering through fields of tall grass, you walk out onto rounded ledge at 2.1 miles. A signpost officially marks this spot as Harmon Hill.

Mount Anthony (2,340 feet) rises above Bennington, which spreads below to the west. The city's historic battle monument towers pointedly from its center. Glastenbury Mountain is the 3,748-foot giant to the northeast. Almost due north, and closer, is Bald Mountain. Trees rim the other exposures of the summit and obstruct views in those directions.

Your return is by the same route.

11

Mount Olga

Class: II
Distance (round trip): 1.5 miles
Hiking time: 1 hour
Vertical rise: 515 feet
USGS 15' Wilmington

Camping –
Molly Stark
State Park

The hiking trail to Mount Olga begins in Molly Stark State Park in Wilmington. Molly Stark gave vital and historic aid to her husband, General John Stark, during the Battle of Bennington in 1777. In the first week of August of that year she received an urgent missive from the General:

"Dear Molly: In less than a week, the British forces will be ours. Send every man from the farm that will come and let the haying go."

In addition to the men from their own farm, Molly rounded up two hundred others to join General Stark in battle. For her reward, she received one of the six brass cannons the triumphant Americans captured from the British during the battle.* (The Molly Stark Cannon is now displayed in the New Boston, New Hampshire, town library.)

The mountain you climb on this hike is also named for a woman of generous spirit. Olga Haslund deeded the peak to the State of Vermont with the understanding that it would be called after her.

*From a brochure on Molly State Park; Vermont Department of Forests and Parks.

To reach Molly Stark State Park, drive east on VT 9 (The Molly Stark Trail) for 3.4 miles from the junction of VT 9 and VT 100 in Wilmington. There is a green state park sign at the entrance. Make your way to the administration building to pay your 50¢ per-person-per-day facilities fees. Then follow the sign to the parking area. If you are taking any dogs with you on this hike, the park asks that you have them on a leash not more than seven feet long. You should also note that this park closes during the first week in October.

Follow the grassy road that starts to the left front of the administration building and travels south to a small clearing and a trail junction. Here bear left, following the sign for Mount Olga. (The white-blazed Ghost Trail to the right leads to the park's camping and picnic area and has been specifically designed as a short and easy hike.)

Follow the blue markers .2 mile to another trail junction. Here a sign points left to "fire tower." Go left onto the blue-blazed trail, which leads to the fire tower on Mount Olga's summit. (The way right is the Stone Wall Trail, which also runs to the park's camping and picnic area.)

A representative inhabitant of this

area is the distinctively plumed barred owl. Its head, neck, and upper breast feathers form dark bars across a lighter colored background. Since this owl's small feet are not large enough to capture sizable prey, its diet consists mainly of mice—which it catches in open country near its home deep in the woods.

Try answering the barred owl's call (four evenly pitched hoots, then the same repeated), or make a squeaking sound with your mouth against the back of your hand. One of these large, inquisitive birds may appear in a nearby tree at any time of day to inspect you carefully with its dark brown eyes.

The wider blue-blazed trail leads upward more steeply. Occasionally you have to scramble around rocks or small boulders. On either side of the path are open deciduous forests dominated by beech trees.

After slabbing the slope to the left, the way levels out and passes between two giant sections of ledge. Becoming narrower, the path passes red blazes on the right at .6 mile. These mark the boundary line of Molly Stark State Park.

The path frequently twists and turns through short evergreens as it approaches the top of Mount Olga. Just below the summit a blue-blazed trail joins from the left. This will be your return route. Go right to an old road and turn right again. Follow this road to the top (2,415 feet).

Transmitting antennae, three small buildings, and a fire tower crowd the small, open summit. From the tower you can scan the surrounding countryside in all directions. Three peaks are particularly prominent. Hogback Mountain (2,410 feet) is in the near northeast. To the northwest is 3,425-foot Haystack Mountain, and 3,556-foot Mount Snow is to the north-northwest.

Follow the path back down the old road and left to the junction of the two blue-blazed trails. Go right here. Your descent, though moderately steep at times, is cushioned by the evergreen spills that thickly cover the path. The trail sides are filled with spruce and balsam fir.

Along the trail to Mount Olga

At 1.1 miles the way leads through a stone wall. This is still a quietly pretty trail. The sound of your steps is muffled by the needles covering the path. The light filters softly through thick branches.

At 1.2 miles this trail intersects an unused footpath that joins from the left. Go right here and continue down the slope. In contrast to the deciduous woods you passed through on the way up, the return route has meandered down through a seemingly endless evergreen forest. Small, bushy "youngsters" are scattered amongst the taller, slimmer parent trees. There are also a few thick-trunked "grandparent" spruces.

At 1.4 miles you cut through another stone wall. Soon you cross a wooden-planked bridge over a small brook. The trail then steps up to the park road just across from the administration building.

12

Haystack Mountain

Class: III
Distance (round trip): 2.4 miles
Hiking time: 1 1/2 hours
Vertical rise: 1,242 feet
USGS 15' Wilmington

Prepare for a picnic—and a sun-soaking—on the summit of Haystack Mountain. A brief but rugged ascent takes you to its small, evergreen-enclosed peak.

You begin using your "path finding" skills early as you search for the start of the Haystack Mountain Trail. Some years back there was a fairly direct route from VT 9 north to the trail. However, the spread of civilization in general and the rise of a community of new houses and roads in particular make finding the trailhead a bit more challenging today.

From the junction of VT 100 and VT 9 in Wilmington, drive west on VT 9. After 1.1 miles, turn north onto Haystack Road at the Chimney Hill sign. Follow this road for 1.2 miles to another Chimney Hill sign. Turn left here onto Chimney Hill Road.

Take the next right onto Binney Brook Road. Follow its turning, angling route past Howe's Loop, Large Maple Way, Lila Lane, and the upper end of Howe's Loop. At the *T* intersection with Twin Chimney Road go right and continue to the next T intersection. Go left onto Upper Dam Road. Drive past Rocky Split Way and another (unnamed) paved road.

Just beyond it, on the right, the Haystack Mountain Trail begins as a dirt road. Park along the edge of the wider section of the paved road.

A small brown yellow-arrowed sign directs you up the old dirt road as it leads away from Upper Dam Road at a 30-degree angle. A remarkably friendly group of chickadees may herald your arrival. Whistle their chick-a-dee notes, and they may venture closer for a noisy inspection. You may see both the black-capped and the smaller, brown-capped species, although the brown-capped chickadees favor higher elevations. Both species prefer to nest in natural cavities or old woodpecker holes in rotten stumps. They feed primarily on insects.

The old dirt road climbs moderately from Upper Dam Road. Although somewhat rutted and rocky, it is smooth enough to let you set a rhythmic pace. At about .1 mile another old road joins from the right. Continue straight and make your way around or under the car chain across the road.

There are no blazes to direct you along the occasionally boggy road. However, the way is well cleared, and the narrower trail that ascends to the summit is a well-beaten one. The vertical rise along the road is consistently gradual. At .4 mile the trail swings slightly right. Below the embankment to the left you can see the waters of Binney Brook.

A culvert guides the brook's journey beneath the trail. Beyond this point the slope of the road increases. At .6 mile the road forks right. Bear left at the yellow arrow trail marker onto the narrower trail leading up the mountainside.

This unblazed footpath curls up over rocks and small boulders. Winding to the right, it maintains a steadily demanding pitch, and then, beyond a sharp bend to the left, it becomes even steeper.

Trees protrude from a jutting section of ledge ahead as the trail swings right below it. Continuing up this southern slope of Haystack Mountain, you pass through a section where the trail has gouged and gutted the hillside.

You're likely to see animal droppings atop the small boulders in and around the trail. Weasels are one animal noted for depositing their scats on these rocks. Also, they tend to use the same spot again and again, so there may be both old and new accumulations. There will be pieces of fur and bone in their slender two-inch droppings.

Nearing the summit, you pass through an area fragrant with evergreens and glistening with birches. Shortly before reaching the top, the needle-covered trail levels out and bears sharply right.

You emerge onto the summit at 1.2 miles. The small, ledged area nestles within a circle of evergreens. Rocks warmed by the sun invite you to stretch out and warm yourself too. Climb up onto the highest piece of ledge to examine the views. Over and between the trees you can see 3,556-foot Mount Snow to the north. Wide, bare swaths of ski trails scar its slopes. The lofty blue shape on the northeast horizon is Mount Ascutney. Directly below, to the northeast, is Haystack Pond. This is the water supply for the town of Wilmington.

Far to the east you can see New Hampshire's 3,165-foot Monadnock Mountain. To the south is Harriman Reservoir. In the distant southeast is 3,491-foot Mount Greylock, the highest point in Massachusetts. Much of the view to the west and north is blocked by trees.

When you are ready to return, remember to bear left at the fork as you step down off the summit. Then follow the same route by which you ascended.

13

Bald Mountain (Townshend State Forest)

Class: III
Distance (round trip): 2.7 miles
Hiking time: 3 hours
Vertical rise: 1,140 feet
USGS 15' Saxtons River

"Bald" is by far the most popular name for Vermont's treeless peaks. Whatever the reason for such popularity, Vermont's "Bald Mountains" must be further identified by their geographical locations. This hike takes you to the summit of 1,680-foot Bald Mountain in the Townshend State Forest in the southeastern quarter of the state.

The short, steep climb to this peak will challenge those in above-average physical condition. If you are not in good shape, this climb could be downright humiliating and possibly unwise to attempt. The trail rises 1,140 feet in only .8 mile.

On VT 30 drive 2.5 miles south from the steepled white church in West Townshend or 2 miles north from the junction of VT 30 and VT 35 in Townshend. Go west onto the narrow steel bridge at the Townshend Dam. This impressive structure was built between 1959 and 1961 by the U.S. Army Corps of Engineers to control flood waters in the Connecticut River Basin. It is operated for the protection of downstream areas in Vermont, New Hampshire, Massachusetts, and Connecticut. During the record storms of June 30-July 4, 1973, it held back millions of gallons of water, thereby preventing possible loss of life and heavy damage in downstream communities.

Follow the road over the bridge and dam to its end and go left. Just before turning sharply right the road approaches the Scott Covered Bridge. Built in 1870, this is the longest single span (165.7 feet) of its type in Vermont.

Turn right at the main entrance of the Townshend State Forest Camping Area (1.7 miles from the dam). Park in the big lot that appears on your right as you approach the main building. Stop in at the office and pay your 50¢ per-person, per-day use fee and ask for the state forest pamphlet for the hiking trail to Bald Mountain. Note that no pets are allowed in this state forest, and that it is officially open only from Memorial Day to Columbus Day.

The short steep climb begins just behind the main building. It passes a large, solitary stone fireplace on the left and heads upward. Rocks and roots slow your pace as you begin to feel the angle of the slope. Follow the blue blazes.

At .2 mile the trail crosses an overgrown path. The forested areas here are very young. Most of the trees are slender light grey beeches.

The trail turns sharply right at .3 mile

and then almost immediately left and resumes its upward climb. Approaching thick stands of evergreens, the grade becomes even steeper. The incline rather than the footing is what makes progress so laborious.

Tall hemlocks with occasional white birches spotting the green fill this unusual area. The dark roughness of tree trunks and cold greyness of ledge are softened by gentle green hemlock needles.

Small spruces line the trail as it levels out at 6 mile. Legs and lungs receive a short rest before the trail swings left and up once again. The last .2 mile to the top is a little less steep but climbs over more ledge and large boulders.

Throughout this climb you will see small ground-level caves dotting the hillside. Formed by rocks piled together, they provide ideal homes for porcupines.

The flat summit is composed of ledge and grass. To the right is an open vista looking northwest. Stratton Mountain dominates the left side of this view. Return to the trail and follow the sign to the south vista. Actually looking southeast, you peer down into the valley of the West River. Across a high ridge line are tiny distant peaks. New Hampshire mountains poke their heads up on the left horizon.

Follow the blue blazes down the more gentle south side of the mountain. The path steepens somewhat and then flattens out. White pine needles cushion the way.

Approximately .2 mile from the summit the trail passes an alder swamp behind you and off the trail on the left. These trees, which are closely related to the birches, have white cross marks on their brown bark. In the eastern United States they are shrub or small tree size. The leaves have short stems and strong, slanted veins. Beavers use alders for both food and building materials.

View of Scott Covered Bridge and Bald Mountain

The trail narrows and passes down through a lane of tall, scraggly pines. Then, at 1.4 miles, you step over the cut pieces of a once-mighty white birch whose six main branches were each "tree size."

Descending easily, the trail reaches the red-blazed line of boundary markers for the state forest. Staying on state land, the path makes a sweeping turn to the right and passes through the opening in an old, moss-greened stone wall.

Just beyond are a number of tamaracks. Also known as larches, these conifers lose their leaves in the fall. Their inch-long needles grow in tufts at the end of dwarfed branchlets and have a furry look. The tamarack's seeds, inner bark, and needles provide food for a variety of woodland creatures.

Passing through more evergreens, the trail begins a long, fairly steep descent to the brook below. It swings right and parallels the water before crossing it at 2.1 miles.

Don't be surprised if you see trees with exceptionally large leaves through this area. The basswood linden has eight-inch leaves that are sharply-toothed and unequally heart-shaped at the base. This is a tree with many by-products. Its soft wood is used for excelsior and lumber. American Indians made rope from the rough inner bark and medicinal tea from the fruit. The flowers are a good source of honey.

The trail continues its descent beside the brook. At 2.5 miles it crosses back to the other side and joins with a dirt road. Go right at the fork here and return to your car.

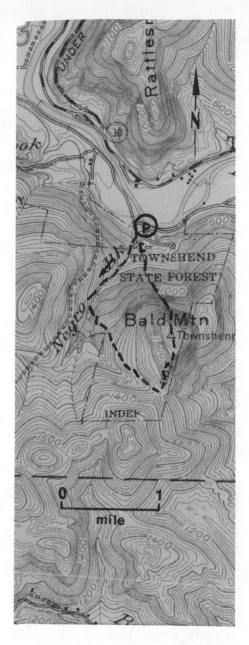

14

Mount Equinox

Class: IV
Distance (round trip): 6 miles
Hiking time: 4 hours
Vertical rise: 2,861 feet
USGS 7.5' Manchester

Many legends have been handed down about this mountain's name. A popular but fictitious one centered around Captain Partridge, one-time director of the American Literary and Scientific Academy. During the autumnal equinox on September 19, 1832, the captain marched a group of cadets to the summit, where they conducted barometric measurements. Most probably, Equinox derives from the Indian word "Ewanok" meaning "the-place-where-the-top-is."

Mount Equinox is the highest mountain in Vermont not on or adjacent to the Long Trail. At more than 3,800 feet it is also the highest peak overlooking the Vermont Valley, which extends from Bennington to Rutland.

Because of malaria in the lowlands and the Indians' fear of high mountains, nineteenth-century settlers populated the slopes of Equinox. During those times the mountain teemed with trails. Lack of interest and need, however, have allowed them to become overgrown. Today the Burr and Burton Trail ascends directly from the valley to the summit. (Two others connect the Sky Line Drive Toll Road with Lookout Rock.)

The climb up the Burr and Burton Trail begins gradually but soon becomes

challenging, so you'll want to be physically ready for this one before starting out. Legs will seldom get a rest, and many trees cross the trail, forcing you to climb over or crawl under them. The path is well marked near the bottom, but the blue blazes disappear as you go higher.

To reach the trailhead from Manchester, drive north on US 7. Take the first left onto Seminary Road. Follow it to the front of Burr and Burton Seminary. Continue on Seminary Road as it bears around to the left. Take the next right into the driveway that leads up behind the school into a large parking area.

Climb up to the athletic field above the parking area. Cross to the far side toward the left corner and watch for the well-beaten path. Unsigned but blue-blazed, the Burr and Burton Trail begins here.

The flat, needle-covered trail winds gradually upward beneath white pines. It joins an old road and continues straight. As the incline steepens, a yellow-blazed path exits left. The rutted road forks at .4 mile, and the trail goes left. Climbing the moderate slope, you switch back to the right and cross an intersecting road at .6 mile.

Thick stands of striped maple line the way. At the next fork, at .7 mile, follow the trail left. Another path joins from the left rear before you bear right at the next fork.

You can now forget about watching for forks in the trail and turn your attention to the running ground pine along the path's edges. This creeping evergreen is actually a club moss. It is used for Christmas decorations and is commonly referred to as princess pine.

As the trail switches back to the left and loops widely right, its pitch increases. From here to the summit, you are in for a relentless uphill trek. Passing through many white birches, the path makes a long traverse up to the left. It narrows suddenly and squeezes past a glacial boulder at 1.3 miles. Quickly returning to its wider ways, it again climbs steadily.

Evergreens cloak the hillsides as the path begins a wide swing to the right. Footing becomes less sure as it narrows. The slope steepens even more. The sides of the trail rise as it turns right. This rock-filled shallow gully is a haven for lush greens. Mosses, lichens, and ferns fill the evergreen-shaded path.

After a series of short turns the trail makes a long, steep climb to the left. At 2.1 miles it ends the sharp uphill pitch and bends slowly right. It becomes surprisingly gradual before gaining elevation again.

Make your way up through body-brushing balsams past the "NO TRESPASSING" signs (these apply not to hikers but to hunters, trappers, and people carrying firearms). Just beyond, at 2.5 miles, several trails intersect. At the first fork bear left; at the second fork pass the red trail and follow the yellow trail. The next .2 mile to the summit passes through evergreens. You cross an old road at 2.6 miles and climb to the junction with the Lookout Rock Trail. Go left across the open ledge to the summit. Ahead is the Equinox Sky Line Inn.

By circling the inn you can see for miles in all directions. On the far horizon you can look into New York State, Massachusetts, and New Hampshire. On a clear day, Mont Royal in Montreal, Canada, is also said to be faintly visible.

Looking north and east you can see Dorset Peak, Killington Peak, Bromley Mountain, Magic Mountain, and Mount Ascutney. To the south, Stratton Mountain, Mount Snow, and Glastenbury Mountain are prominent. The Adiron-

View from summit of Mount Equinox

dacks rise to the west.

Also located on the summit are Federal Aviation Agency peripheral communications stations. These radio towers enable planes to contact Boston's Logan Airport for landing instructions. An educational television station erected by the University of Vermont transmits near the Lookout Rock Trail.

When you are ready to descend, return to the Lookout Rock Trail and follow it .4 mile to Lookout Rock. This is a fairly easy walk over some rock and through evergreens. A small clearing along the way contains a memorial to Mr. Barbo, the dog of Dr. J.G. Davidson, former owner and developer of much land on Mount Equinox.

From Lookout Rock you gaze down into the Vermont Valley. Stratton Mountain looms to the right and Equinox Pond sits directly below you.

Leaving this vantage point, bear left onto the yellow trail and follow it .4 mile to the junction with the Burr and Burton Trail. Turn sharply left onto this unsigned trail and return via your original route to your car.

15

Bromley Mountain + *Bromley Brook*

Class: III
Distance (round trip): 4.6 miles
Hiking time: 2 1/2 hours
Vertical rise: 1,320 feet
USGS 15' Londonderry

This is a two-in-one hike. The greater part, two-thirds of the way up Bromley Mountain, is a gentle woodland walk. The last third is a steeper, slower climb. You can meander or stride for about 1.5 miles before settling into the more arduous, muscle-tugging final climb of .7 mile.

The trail to Bromley Mountain begins at the Long Trail crossing of the Manchester-Peru Highway (VT 11). Drive east 5.9 miles from Manchester Center or west 4.4 miles from Peru. Turn north at the Green Mountain National Forest sign and park in the paved parking lot.

Walk approximately 150 yards down the road. At the sign for the Long Trail turn left into the woods. Follow the well-beaten path across the steel footbridge over Bromley Brook. The white-blazed trail leads very gradually upward. Cut logs carry you across a wet area as the ground flattens out. Step over the thin, weaving roots and small rocks that fill the path. Sounds of moving water can be heard to the left. As you continue, the rock-floored brook comes into view. Flashes of white water highlight its swirling, downward journey.

To the sides of the trail are the ever-present dead or dying trees that form an integral part of the forest's life cycle. They serve as hosts for various types of fungi—nonflowering plants that lack the chlorophyll necessary for photosynthesis and thus depend upon other organisms for food.

You can see examples of the rusty-hoof fome that attaches itself primarily to beech and birch trees. This three-to twelve-inch wide, cone-shaped fungus is a perennial that may grow for as long as thirty-five years. With each new year it adds a zone of tubes, called pore fungi, located on the plant's sheltered underside.

Walking gradually upward to the right, you reach another crossing of Bromley Brook at .6 mile. A raised, cross-logged footbridge provides rustic support here. Rising up from the brook the trail becomes very flat as it winds through open woodlands. Occasional glacial boulders loom mutely among the trees, their great bulks harboring the many greens of ferns, mosses, and trees.

The way leads past a wide, gentle rock-free section of Bromley Brook on the right. A three-logged bridge carries you over a small streamlet on its way to the brook. As you pass through this area, you must step over several other trickles of water.

At 1.3 miles a small hump of ledge interrupts the flatness of the path. The bright whiteness of this quartz-filled rock contrasts sharply with the dull brown of the packed dirt path.

Watch for pleurotus mushrooms growing on living trees (they never grow on the ground). The oyster pleurotus grows in tight clusters and has three-to five-inch flared caps, one above the other. Gills form riblike undersides. This mushroom is usually white or grey when young and becomes yellowish with age. We do not recommend sampling any of the mushrooms described. Many edible and poisonous species look so much alike it is nearly impossible to tell them apart.

The trail approaches the brook again at 1.6 miles and then swings away to the left. Your first taste of the steep climb that will bring you to the top lies just ahead. After cresting a short ridge and temporarily leaving out, the path begins a serious ascent.

The way narrows as it begins the long climb. Thick birches, maples, and beeches staunchly guard the edges of the twisting trail. Huge boulders lean out from the hillside above as you climb diagonally to the right. Cresting the ridge, the path swings left across it and readies itself for the heights ahead. Rising steeply again, the trail passes through predominantly beech forests. It tops this ridge and flattens out once again.

The hairy woodpecker is common here. This black and white bird has a white breast and vertical stripes down its back. (The male displays a small red

Bridge over Bromley Brook

patch on the back of his head.) Its barb-tipped tongue can be extended into holes to reach the larvae of boring beetles. Not to be confused with the smaller, but similarly marked downy woodpecker (six to seven inches long), the hairy woodpecker (eight to nine inches long), has a much longer, heavier bill, and it dwells primarily in forests.

Just before reaching a ski slope at 2.2 miles, the path crosses an unusual jumble of smooth-topped rocks. Look right (south) when you walk out onto the ski slope for a beautifully framed view of Stratton Mountain (elevation, 3,936 feet).

Turn left and follow the steep ski trail to the top of Bromley Mountain. A sturdy wooden observation tower offers fine views in all direction. Close to the north is Styles Peak. Looking east you see many low rolling hills, with no outstanding peaks. Stratton Mountain is prominent in the south, and the high peak in the distance to the southwest is Glastenbury Mountain. The Taconic Range looms impressively to the west. Hotel-topped Mount Equinox dominates the near west.

Your return will be by the same route.

16

Baker Peak and Griffith Lake

Class: III
Distance (round trip): 7.4 miles
Hiking time: 4 hours
Vertical rise: 2,130 feet
USGS 15' Wallingford

This hike takes you through an area that was quite exclusive in earlier times. Vermont's first millionaire, Silas Griffith, built a lake house retreat on the body of water that now bears his name. He made his fortune lumbering the forests around the nearby town of Danby, although the town itself did not take on an air of prosperity until quarrying and dairy farming became established in the 1800s.

Expansive views from the summit of Baker Peak and a peaceful visit to the wilderness shores of Griffith Lake highlight this outing. The mileage makes this trek a real leg-stretcher, but there are no sections of tedious climbing. Even the approach over open ledges to Baker Peak can be handled easily.

Drive 2 miles south from Danby on US 7. Turn east onto a paved road next to a small cemetery. Follow this road for .5 mile to the Green Mountain National Forest sign for the Lake Trail, on the left. There is ample parking in an open field beside the sign.

Your walk begins on the Lake Trail and then branches off onto the Baker Peak Trail. After leaving the summit of Baker Peak, you'll walk the Long Trail south to Griffith Lake. The Lake Trail will return you to the parking area.

The blue-blazed Lake Trail leads right from the field where you parked and follows the old carriage road that leads from the valley to Griffith's lake retreat. Pine needles cloak the trail here as it leads gradually upward. You can hear the loud rushing of McGinn Brook below the hillside to the left. After the initial gradual incline the trail levels out, and at .2 mile it dips down to cross a fast-flowing brook, whose left bank it then parallels.

The area between the .3- and about .8-mile marks was being logged when the revised edition of this guide went to press (1981). It was not particularly attractive nor easy to follow. You may have to watch very carefully for the blue blazes that mark your route. At .6 mile the path makes a rounded switchback to the left. Look for a brown sign with a yellow arrow pointing your way. This is the start of a long upward traverse.

The hillsides rise high above and drop off steeply below. Smooth ledges form occasional walls above the trail. At 1.2 miles a bridge carries you across a gap beneath one of these steep stone faces.

The supports of an old trestle can be seen imbedded in the rock below. Beyond the bridge the trail continues to traverse the slope. Steadily climbing, it narrows and passes along a hillside flooded with white birches.

The way swings right, still curling around the hillside's edge. McGinn Brook's gushing becomes audible far below, but its frothy white waters settle into quiet pools where the trail comes to meet the stream. At 1.5 miles you reach Ben's Bathtub, one of the larger pools along the trail. This lovely spot invites you to refresh yourself before traveling on.

You reach a trail junction just after you cross McGinn Brook at 1.6 miles. The Lake Trail leads right and the Baker Peak Trail, left. Go left onto the blue-blazed Baker Peak Trail, which makes a long, moderate climb along the mountain's western slope. The narrow path passes between brilliant slopes of white birches and leads just below the ridge line. Then, swinging sharply right, it passes over rougher sections of loose rock and protruding roots. The trail becomes more gradual as it curves through thick stands of dwarfed birches.

At 2.4 miles you reach open ledge. Looking left you can see US 7 in the valley below. Dorset Peak, with its white quarries, rises commandingly beyond the highway. The quarries were first worked in the early 1800s. At that time the demand was for relatively small cut stones to be used for hearths, doorsteps, and tombstones. With the advent of better transportation and equipment, larger stones were quarried.

The Baker Peak and Long Trails join at 2.5 miles. Their blue and white blazes follow the same route the final 500 feet to the summit. Just beyond this junction is the Bad Weather Bypass. This sheltered route is recommended when inclement weather makes the climb over open rocks hazardous.

The final ascent is a steady climb over a wide, smooth spine of rippled ledge. To your left is a tantalizing preview of the wide western view you'll witness at the top. The summit is a tiny flattened area identified by a painted blue square. A sign just beyond marks Baker Peak's elevation at 2,850 feet.

The view extends through 180 degrees of the compass. In clear weather, sharp-peaked Killington and the

Along the Lake Trail

rounded cone of Pico can be seen to the north. The Adirondacks are partially visible to the northwest. Dorset Peak is directly across, with Woodlawn Mountain behind to the right. Emerald Lake sparkles to the south. Netop Mountain and Green Peak back it up, while Equinox Mountain raises its lofty head just beyond. Looking down into the valley, you see the town of Danby to the northwest. US 7 slices the valley floor in a north-south direction, and the looping bends to its east are Otter Creek.

Return to the junction of the Baker Peak and Long Trails. Go left onto the Long Trail South. This route is consistently easy going. Level stretches alternate with gradual dips and rises. At 3.3 miles you begin the first noticeable ascent as the path brushes by a large glacial boulder. At 3.6 miles you cross a damp, boggy area via the raised roots of nearby trees.

The Long Trail intersects with the Lake Trail at 4.3 miles and swings left. Follow it approximately 500 feet through evergreens and birches to the northern

end of Griffith Lake. Sunlight dances on the water's surface as you approach. After passing the Old Job Trail on the left you reach the lake's shore. This quiet, primitive setting is an ideal spot to eat lunch and spend some time just lazing around.

When ready, retrace your steps on the Long Trail to its junction with the Lake Trail. Go straight on the blue-blazed Lake Trail. The path flattens out as it passes through a grassy field. It then crosses two tiny brooks and makes a sharp swing to the left. At 5.2 miles the trail bears left onto an old rutted road, which it follows for approximately .5 mile down a long, gradual grade, crossing several tiny brooks in the process.

The road narrows to trail width as rushing brooks accompany it on both sides. They meet and swing left as the path crosses over them and shortly thereafter intersects the Baker Peak Trail. Go straight, across McGinn Brook, and follow your original route back to your car.

17

Mount Antone

Class: II
Distance (round trip): 4.6 miles
Hiking time: 2 1/2 hours
Vertical rise: 850 feet
USGS 7.5' Pawlet

Mount Antone lies within the boundaries of Merck Forest (see also Hike 2). This unique woodland and forest area contains twenty-six miles of hiking and cross-country ski trails for public use. Nine overnight shelters and many picnic sites are also scattered throughout the forest. There is no charge for visiting the forest, which is run by a private foundation, but contributions are appreciated. Any money received is applied to future recreational and educational goals. Visitors are requested to obey the forest's rules, however:

1. All visitors must register.
2. No motor vehicles are allowed beyond the parking area.
3. Camping is by permit only.
4. Fires are allowed only in designated areas.
5. All trash must be carried out.
6. Hunting and fishing are permitted, but kills must be reported.
7. Only snowshoers and cross-country skiers may use the forest in the winter.

The entrance to Merck Forest is located on VT 315 at the height-of-land between Rupert and East Rupert. Drive east 3.3 miles from the junction of VT

153 in Rupert, or west 2.6 miles from the junction of VT 30 and VT 315 in East Rupert. Turn south toward the brown and yellow "Merck Forest Foundation, Inc." sign. When the entrance road forks, bear right and go .5 mile to the parking area, on the right.

Walk the short distance to the information board, and register. Maps of the forest are also available here. Now go through the log swing gate next to the information board and begin your hike down Old Town Road. White birches surround you as the road leads gradually upward. In about .2 mile you come to a junction—there's a large barn on the right. Bear right to stay on Old Town Road.

The trail dips between large patches of cleared land. Down to the right is Page Pond. You're likely to hear the quacking of wild ducks echoing from this tiny body of water. Just beyond the pond you can look up to the right and see the humped dome of Mount Antone. You head up a slight rise, where young trees begin to fill the hillside to the left. Open land to the right allows for an excellent view to the northwest.

Young forests cloak both sides of the trail as it continues to rise gradually and then flattens out. Continued easy walking brings you to a sweeping left turn at .8 mile. Follow the curve to the clearing, where several trails radiate outward. Before turning sharply right to follow the footpath leading to Mount Antone's summit, walk to the far edge of this cleared area. From here you can see Mount Equinox, with its summit hotel and transmitting towers.

Follow the grassy trail next to the Mount Antone Road sign. Look carefully; it's just off to the right when you reach the clearing. On the left you'll see a stand of red pines, with their characteristically uplifted branches. This northern tree has three-to eight-inch needles in clusters of two.

Gentle dips and rises make for easy walking as the trail passes through hardwood forests. Many thin, young, grey-barked beeches cover this area. At 1.1 miles you pass through Clark Clearing. Another clearing just beyond offers distant views west to the Adirondacks of New York State.

A quaint four-sided cabin comes into view on the right. Built of logs and set atop a stone foundation, it has tall, narrow windows fashioned by leaving out vertical logs in appropriate places. Stumps and flat stones make the inside comfortable, while a front overhang keeps rain from the open door.

In front of the cabin is a four-way trail junction. The Mount Antone Road leads diagonally upward to the right (but just to the left of a ski-touring trail). The steeper part of the hike begins here. You cut up to the left across a slope and turn right. A series of turns brings you to the crest of the ridge. The trail remains

White birches

smooth and easy to walk through here, but the incline does offer some challenge.

The trail flattens out and crosses the ridge to the right. Just ahead, at 1.8 miles, the ski-touring trail rejoins from the right. Continue straight on the Mount Antone Road when the Wade Lot Road branches left. In another 500 feet you pass Lookout Road. The trail then bends around a small knoll on the right and begins a long, straight, gradual ascent.

At 2.1 miles you reach a sweeping switchback to the right. Leading left from the turn are the Beebe Pond Trail and Masters Mountain Road. The grade is now steeper as you climb to the summit.

You enter the small, flat area at the top of Mount Antone 2.3 miles from the information center. To the right (northeast) you overlook much of Merck Forest. The barn you passed earlier is visible in the large clearing straight ahead. The three towering summits beyond are (from right to left): Dorset Peak, Woodlawn Mountain, and Tinmouth Mountain.

A narrow path leads off the far side of the clearing. Follow this a short distance to another cleared overlook. From here you look down into the valley to the fields of scattered farms and out across low, rolling hills. On a clear day it is possible to see westward as far as the Adirondack peaks of Mount Marcy and Whiteface Mountain.

On the return trip, take the ski-touring trail, which branches off to the left after .5 mile. It descends moderately and straight along the side of the slope and will bring you back to the cabin. Remember to bear left here and then hike back to the information center by the route you came up. If you enjoyed this trek, why not plan to return to Merck Forest in winter for some excellent cross-country skiing?

18

Natural Bridge

Class: III
Distance (round trip): 3.5 miles
Hiking time: 1 3/4 hours
Vertical rise: 840 feet
USGS 7.5' Dorset

Imagine a deep gorge carved into solid rock by the relentless rushing of cascading water. Ragged edges show where rocks have broken away, and the sides of the crevice flare freely upward—with one exception. Somehow a slender span of rock has failed to crumble. It connects the sides of the gorge like a narrow catwalk. This is the natural bridge.

Don't be misled by the shortness of this hike. It is a rugged climb. The trail itself is easy to walk, but the steep incline keeps you leaning into the hill most of the way. Be ready for a good workout. However, the many breathers that your heart, lungs, and legs will insist upon, should provide excellent opportunities to observe the abundant plant and animal life of this area.

To reach the trailhead, turn west off US 7 in North Dorset onto the entrance road for Emerald Lake State Park. Drive into the park and leave your car in the parking area. You will be asked to pay a nominal fee. Walk back down the road .3 mile and turn left by the white and black state park sign to pick up the trail.

Please note: This trail is on private land, and the property owner has, so far, allowed the public to use it. This permission can be rescinded at any time, so

hikers should help care for the path as they hike.

A gradual slope bordered by open fields offers a pleasant beginning. In the ravine to the left a rushing brook provides musical accompaniment as you wind your way upward. After approximately .2 mile the wide trail forks. Watch closely for the blue blazes to keep you on the main trail. At this fork, keep right and ascend the steep slope ahead. Loose rocks make the pulse-quickening climb even harder.

Hemlocks arch their delicate branches along the path as another trail enters from the right rear. These beautiful trees have more flexible twigs and branches than spruces or balsams, as well as tiny, perfectly formed cones. Their bark is rich in tannin; woodsmen and Indians made tea from the twigs and leaves. A barbed-wire fence parallels the path and seems to divide the forest. White birches abound to the right while evergreens occupy the left. The long, moderate uphill grade continues.

Swinging right, the wide packed-dirt trail becomes steeper. The sides of the path rise higher; your steps become more laborious. Then you crest a long grade and swing sharply left. The grade lessens a bit as the trail makes a long, diagonal switchback to the left.

Rocks fill the trail as it continues relentlessly upward. Looking left through the trees, you can see a ridge line towering high above across a deep valley. The mountains responsible for this high landmark are Dorset Hill, Netop Mountain, and Dorset Peak.

The trail swings sharply left as the hillside suddenly flattens out. The grade lessens. Your legs get a short reprieve.

Red squirrels may chatter at you throughout this area. These vivacious creatures have a very small home range—usually within a small group of trees. They live in hollow trees; or, if these are not available, they build out-side nests of grass and fine twigs and line them with shredded bark. In addition to gathering nuts and cones for winter storage, they place mushrooms high on tree branches to dry in the sun before tucking them away.

You cross a dry brook bed at .8 mile. The trail cuts across the slope here and remains fairly flat. Deer tracks can be seen in the soft dirt. Whitetail deer most often leave separated, two-toed tracks, although sometimes they appear as single, heart shaped prints. You may be fortunate enough to see one of these beautiful creatures or at least its raised white flag (tail) as it runs from you. A sharp snort or whistle will also signal the presence of deer.

Just before the trail begins to rise again, it passes over a jumble of large white limestone rocks. Ferns begin to appear along the sides of the trail. Two unusual kinds grow abundantly here. The maidenhair fern has finely divided horseshoe-shaped leaves. The Christmas fern is slender from base to tip with a scaly leafstalk, stiff leaves, and spiny leaflets.

A wide trail joins from the left rear at 1.1 miles. Note this junction well. On the return trip you must bear left onto the

narrower trail you are now following to return to your car.

Continuing upward, the presence of a stone wall on the right alerts you to the next turn. At the end of the wall, follow the blue blazes steeply downhill to the right. The narrow path leads directly to the natural bridge.

The two-foot-wide stone arch is start-ing to crumble, so do not try to walk out on it. It connects the rocky hillsides above the floor of the gorge. Water flows through here only during the spring runoff.

19

Little Rock Pond and Green Mountain

Class: IV
Distance (round trip): 5.6 miles
Hiking time: 4 1/2 hours
Vertical rise: 1,849 feet
USGS 15' Wallingford

Give yourself plenty of time to enjoy this wilderness pond and mountain. The area teems with wildlife, and you won't want to rush. A quiet wait can reward you with lots of animal sightings. And besides, it's nice to bask in the sun atop the ledges of Green Mountain.

If an overnight stay fits your plans, you can sleep at the Lula Tye Shelter, located on the Long Trail at the southeastern tip of Little Rock Pond. A spring nearby provides fresh water for the six to eight hikers this shelter can accommodate.

You'll reach your destination via the Homer Stone Brook Trail. To get to it turn east off US 7 just south of the South Wallingford Union Congregational Church. Drive .2 mile across a bridge and around a right-hand curve to a red building on the left. This is the South Wallingford Youth Community Center. Park beside it.

The Homer Stone Brook Trail begins behind the next house on the left. (N.B.: No parking is allowed near this house.) Walk up the driveway and around to the right of the house.

The trail starts by following the old South Wallingford-Wallingford Pond Road. The way leads up a moderate grade, flanked by stone walls and open fields. Blue blazes and occasional arrows mark the route.

After .2 mile the road makes a wide swing to the right. Keep on this packed-dirt road and bypass the path leading left at the bend. Maintaining its gradual slope, the road leads up between borderling hemlocks. These evergreens dust the trail with their tiny needles and miniature cones.

Beyond the hemlocks, you pass through an open deciduous forest. A massive, gnarled maple guards the left side of the road as another trail leads left. Stay on the road. Walking is enjoyable up this gradual incline. You make a brief aromatic passage through a small area of hemlock and white pine.

After .6 mile you can hear the rushing waters of Homer Stone Brook below to the right. Follow the road as it bends right and passes by still another trail leading left.

Now the trail parallels the brook. Clear water pours through boulders trying to choke its flow. Rippled pools form among the rocks. Above to the left the hillside slopes steeply around eroded cliffs. Quaking and large-tooth aspen and beech cling tenaciously to the slope.

For a short stretch the brook drops down into a shallow ravine. You can hear it foaming and surging along below the road. Farther along, the road and brook parallel each other at the same level. A new U.S. Forest Service sign points the way. At approximately 1.3 miles you cross the Homer Stone Brook, leaving the South Wallingford-Wallingford Pond Road. Rounded stones help you cross the flowing water.

Bear sharply right after crossing the brook. Walk about 100 feet, turn sharply left, and begin to climb up the gouged-out slope. Very quickly you top a small mound of earth while the trail joins with an old road. Turn left here. Mark this junction well so that you will not pass by it on the return trip.

The grassy road cuts upward and across the slope to the left. Small rocks clutter the path and make progress slow at times. Homer Stone Brook again meets the trail near the top of this long incline.

The trail crosses over the brook and reaches the junction with the Long Trail at 1.9 miles. Go right and follow the white blazes toward Little Rock Pond. A blue-blazed trail appears quickly on the right. Turn here and follow it over rough-hewn logs bridging the brook's northern outlet. Follow the blue blazes along the pond's western shore.

Isolated Little Rock Pond is a resting place for mallards, Canada geese, and other waterfowl during their spring and fall migrations. Approach its shores with care and you may see one of these species before their wary senses make them fly off.

Mallards are bottom feeders. They submerge their upper bodies in shallow water in quest of plant growth. You will see them "tip up," with their tailends pointing skyward. Recognize the drake

Mallards

by his iridescent green head, white neck ring, white-edged blue wing patch, and curled tail feathers. The hen shares the blue wing patch but is dappled in shades of brown.

The large Canada goose has a black neck and a white mark running like a strap from ear to ear beneath its head. These birds feed on pond plants and on the grass or grain of open fields. In flight, they align themselves in various V formations. "Honking" usually signals the approach of their flying wedge long before you can see it.

The path gently dips and rises along the pond's western shore. Ahead you can see a small island. After you pass the point of the pond's northern outlet, with the island still visible ahead of you, the blue-blazed trail to Green Mountain leads right.

The ascent to Green Mountain quickly becomes steep. The narrow dirt path climbs upward through hardwoods. Multi-zoned polystictus (a fungus with a shape and coloration resembling turkey tails) flare from the surface of dead tree limbs at the sides of the trail.

At the 2.3-mile point the path flattens out and descends briefly. It then swings sharply right and continues its winding ascent through thick stands of beeches. The forest floor is cloaked with verdant fern growth.

The way passes over a long rocky spine of ledge at 2.4 miles. To those who share our habits of imagination, this ledge resembles the back of some fairy tale monster. You'll have to hoist yourself up, using both arms and legs, over the continuing series of ledges. There are intermittent views to the east from open-ledged areas as the trail twists through thick, evergreen scrub growth.

At 2.7 miles the path forks. A spur leads right to the West View. Go left here and continue toward the summit. One-tenth of a mile farther you come to the open, rounded ledge at the summit. A blue circle marks the spot. Views include an easterly look to Little Rock Pond below, Homer Stone Mountain, and the smooth, waved crests of other mountains beyond.

Return by the same route.

20

White Rocks Cliff

Class: III
Distance (round trip): 3.2 miles
Hiking time: 2 hours
Vertical rise: 1,622 feet
USGS 15' Wallingford

You are not at White Rocks Cliff when you reach the highest point of this hike. The spur trail to the cliff follows a rugged, .2-mile downhill route. Once there, you'll enjoy a vantage point with panoramic views to the north and west. There is also a near view of one of three distinct limestone rock slides below northwest face of White Rocks Mountain. About the turn of the century, water coursed down the mountain, causing one whole side to slide off.

Drive east on VT 140 from Wallingford. Bear right onto a side road after about 2 miles. Follow it 500 feet to the sign for the "Green Mountain National Forest: White Rocks Picnic Area." Turn right here and proceed straight on this road for .4 mile to picnic area #52 and the parking lot at its end.

You want the blue-blazed Keewaydin Trail, which leads out of the parking lot's far end. This wide trail begins with a gentle walk between picnic tables and two small Forest Service structures. Off to the left you'll hear the sound of a rushing brook. Then the trail swings right, up and away from the brook. White pine have shed their five-fingered needles across the path. After cresting a

rise, you approach a stream and swing left before it.

Now you maintain a steady upward grade through white birch, largetooth aspen, oak, and maple. Below and to the left you can hear the brook again. Look carefully for an opening in the trees. Through it you'll have a limited view of a small but very attractive cascade.

The trail swings right around a thick, shadowy stand of spruce, balsam, and hemlock, and after briefly paralleling the

View of White Rocks Mountain and Cliffs

ridge line to the left cuts up and across it. A short row of "bog logs" has been laid across a mucky section here.

Great glacial boulders loom in the open woods, and loose rocks fill the trail. Step slowly to avoid careless falls. The return to a packed-dirt trail makes the footing more certain. Your legs and feet appreciate this, as there are few other respites from the unvarying upward grade.

At 1.1 miles the Keewaydin Trail joins the Long Trail. Go right onto the Long Trail South. Frequent white blazes guide your way up and down the gentle dips and rises of the west side of a ridge. Stands of spruce and balsam seem to engulf you. Evergreen spills litter the path. You may want to pause along this sheltered trail to enjoy the surrounding quiet and isolation.

At 1.3 miles you reach a small clearing scattered with numerous broken rocks. The blue-blazed White Rocks Cliff Trail leads right. Make your way carefully over the loose rocks scattered down this steep, rugged descent.

The trail changes to packed dirt and continues its steep drop through conifers whose needles color the slope brown. Twisting and turning through large boulders and ledge, the path makes a final descent to the cliff.

Here there are two flat overlooks: one to the north and one to the west. The town of Wallingford is most prominent to the right. Tinmouth Mountain rises straight ahead in the first ridge line. The second, higher ridge line is that of the Adirondacks of New York State.

Directly below you is one of the great white limestone spills. This type of rock is still processed in a nearby plant. It is used as a base for toothpaste and as an ingredient in lead-base paint.

After returning to the parking area via the same route, you may want to explore the White Rock Trail. This blue-blazed path leads southwest from the other end of the parking lot to an outcropping of ledge below White Rocks Cliff. From this vantage point you can see the cliff and all three white rivers of rock that cascaded down the mountainside. The round-trip walk on this .5-mile-long switchbacking trail takes ½ hour.

21

✳ Mount Ascutney

Class: III
Distance (round trip): 6.6 miles
Hiking time: 4 1/2 hours
Vertical rise: 2,370 feet
USGS 15' Claremont, NH — VT

Mount Ascutney has long been a focus of activity. During the French and Indian Wars bounties up to £100 were paid by both the English colonies and the French for enemy scalps. Colonial scalping parties frequented the area around Mount Ascutney and used to climb to its summit to watch for smoke from Indian campfires.

In 1825 the people of Windsor opened the first trail up the mountain—making Ascutney the first American mountain to have an established hiking trail. Later trails and shelters provided sufficient inspiration for James P. Taylor to found the Green Mountain Club and to initiate the blazing of the 262-mile Long Trail. The Long Trail prompted others to create the 2,000-mile Appalachian Trail, which stretches from Maine to Georgia.

Today, Ascutney boasts a 4-mile-long road to the summit (it is said to be one of New England's most scenic highways) and many ski trails. Small-plane and glider pilots use its distinctive shape as a convenient landmark.

Three major trails lead to Mount Ascutney's summit. The Weathersfield Trail, which was recently revised to eliminate some of its rough sections, ascends from the south. The other two routes climb from the northeast; it is on these two that you hike on the loop described here.

The starting points for these two trails are separated by .8 mile of black-topped road. You have the choice of parking where you plan to begin or (as we prefer) parking where you will finish and then walking back along the road to the starting point.

Drive 3.4 miles west on VT 44 from its junction with US 5 in Windsor, and turn diagonally back to the left onto an intersecting road. Follow this for .3 mile to a small house set back on the right. A sign for parking also indicates that guidebooks are for sale here. Another sign on a fencepost marks the Windsor Trail.

The owners of this property have offered portions of their land as parking areas for Mount Ascutney hikers. This is where the hike will end. You may leave your car at the edge of the lawn, under the trees, or in the scrub land further up the road between the white birches. It is expected that in return for this privilege you will take your trash with you when leaving.

Now walk back to the paved road and go left. From here it is .8 mile to the beginning of the Brownsville Trail. At the junction with VT 44 go left. Follow this road to a red brick farmhouse on the right. Just before this house you will spot the Brownsville Trail sign on the left. White blazes mark the trail as it follows the long, flat, well-beaten path up across the open field. Entering the woods the trail suddenly narrows and slithers through thick stands of hemlock. The branches overlap above, forming a natural tunnel.

You are now on the old Norcross Quarry Road. It rises gradually over packed dirt and loose stones. Then the hillsides become very steep to both left and right. Slabbing the mountain, you cross a jumble of rocks flowing down over the trail like a stone waterfall, and continue upward through more hemlock. The incline lessens here but the footing

is less certain as the path becomes filled with loose stones.

Approximately 2.7 miles from your car you pass a section of ledge rising steeply to the left. Water trickles over the rock all year long, forming a giant sheet of ice during the winter months. During the spring runoff it becomes a gorgeous waterfall.

Farther along you will recognize Norcross Quarry by the masses of large rock along the trailsides. Climb the pile to the right for a view of valleys, rolling ridges, and distant peaks. The long, thick wooden remains of a derrick and rusted steel cables evoke the past.

The Norcross Quarry was the most extensive of the four quarries on Mount Ascutney. It produced the sixteen polished columns for the Columbia University Library and the thirty-four

View to Mount Ascutney across the Windsor-Cornish bridge

large columns for Canada's Bank of Montreal. During its several years of operation, however, it did not produce stone completely free of trace iron. Thus, the stone did not weather well, and the quarry's backers went bankrupt.

The trail continues beneath overhanging ledge. It winds steeply upward between more hunks of ledge and turns sharply left and then right. It becomes steeper as thick stands of evergreens gather along the edges.

A sign at 2.1 miles marks the Quarry Top Lookout. The short blue-blazed spur trail leads onto a flat ledged area above Norcross Quarry. From here you have a wide view to the north. Return to the main trail. After passing through thick stands of evergreens you'll see an arrow directing you to a revised route at 2.4 miles. It leads more steeply up the mountain over packed dirt, many rocks, and roots. From here to Knee Lookout the path is a long series of diagonal traverses up the slope.

At 2.8 miles you arrive at Knee Lookout, with a view to the east. Continue to twist and turn another .2 mile up the mountain until you reach a flat grassy area. This is North Peak: elevation 2,660 feet.

Just beyond this peak you have occasional views to the west through dead trees. Particularly prominent to the northwest are the pointed peak of Killington and the cone of Pico.

Trees shorten as you climb steadily upward toward Mount Ascutney's 3,150 foot summit. At 3.6 miles you reach the junction of the Windsor Trail. Keep right.

The Stone Hut remains occupy the clearing 500 feet further on. You can still see the large slabs of granite used to construct the former shelter. Built in 1858 by volunteers, it was destroyed by vandals, rebuilt in the early 1900s, but later destroyed again—primarily by college students, who carved their initials in the metal roof with pistol bullets.

Leading to the right from this clearing is Brownsville Rock. From here you have a long view to the west and north. Open farmlands sectioned off by trees rise to mountain bases. Mount Mansfield and Camel's Hump are visible far to the north, while the Coolidge Range shows up clearly almost straight ahead. A bit south is Shrewsbury Peak. Salt Ash and Okemo mountains are the closer peaks to the left.

Return to the clearing and go right .3

mile to the summit. A lookout tower and accompanying horde of antennae greet you as you crest the last ledged area. Climb the tower for a fine 360-degree view of the surrounding countryside.

From the summit it is 2.6 miles back to your car. Walk back down the Windsor Trail junction and go right. The way twists and turns through stands of evergreens and scrubby birches to the junction with Blood Rock Trail; you have now traveled a total of 4.7 miles. Keep left on the Windsor Trail.

Becoming rock-free, the path cuts across the slope and switches back to the right. It traverses the mountain and comes to another junction. Go left toward the Log Shelter. This rustic structure was built in 1968 by members of the Ascutney Trails Association. Two sides of the three-sided shelter are built of logs and the third is ledge and stone. It has three wire-bottomed bunks, a fireplace, and a picnic table. Spring water in front completes the natural setting.

You reach Half Way Spring and a second junction of the Blood Rock and Windsor trails after 5.2 miles. The spring water is said to remain constant at a temperature of 39 degrees Fahrenheit.

After a long series of traverses, the trail becomes more gradual. It passes between thick stands of slender maples and becomes filled with loose rocks. The pitch increases as you descend to Mountain Brook at the 5.5-mile mark.

Swinging left, the trail parallels the brook on the right. It descends long hunks and slabs of stone as the brook drops lower into the ravine. Continuing beside the brook, the trail begins a long, straight, moderate descent.

The loose rocks disappear as the path widens. Sides of the path open momentarily and become filled with fluffy white pines. At 6.5 miles, a grassy road goes straight and the trail forks right. You are now just a short walk through blazing white birches from you car.

22

Quechee Gorge

Class: II
Distance (round trip): 1.5 miles
Hiking time: 1 hour
Vertical rise: 125 feet
USGS 7.5' Quechee

Quechee Gorge, Vermont's "Little Grand Canyon," was carved by the waters of the Ottauquechee River. In the middle 1800s the gorge and a nearby area with a steep grade impeded construction of the Woodstock Railroad, planned to link White River Junction and Rutland. Finally, in 1875, twenty-eight years after the Woodstock Railroad was originally chartered, ways were found to overcome these two natural barriers: passengers were enlisted to help push the train cars up the incline, and the gorge was spanned by a 282-foot trestle, crossing 165 feet above the river.

For years the Woodstock Railroad trestle was the highest railroad bridge in New England. Now recycled, it is used as the US 4 highway bridge, crossing the gorge 6 miles east of Woodstock and 5 miles west of White River Junction. The view from the highway bridge can be easily reached by car, but it will be far more rewarding after a walk along the Quechee Gorge Trail.

On US 4, .3 mile east of the gorge, you will see the sign for the Quechee State Park entrance. Turn into the entrance on the south side of the road and proceed along the dirt road for .2 mile.

Park your car at the small area on the right near a "Firewood" sign. Cross the road to the firewood area, and look for the Quechee Gorge Trail sign at the rear of this clearing. Blue blazes mark the way. (Please note that here, as at most Vermont state parks, all dogs must be kept on a leash.)

A delicious pine odor engulfs you momentarily as you approach the trail but disappears quickly as the pines are replaced by hemlocks. Tiny cones and red-brown needles blanket the flat meandering woodland trail.

At approximately .2 mile the trail veers sharply to the right and descends a steep grade through stands of white birch and hemlock. This descent terminates in a small gully at the .3-mile mark. After climbing out of the gully, the trail again drops, this time to a small brook.

The water's whispery gurgle interrupts the quiet of the glen. Roots traversing the trail form natural steps down to the water. Cross the brook on logs furry with moss. Beyond the stream the path rises steeply once again, bearing sharply to the right at the top of the grade.

At approximately .5 mile, you cross a

medium-sized stream tumbling from right to left. The trail climbs a small embankment beyond and levels out once again. The way is miry and strewn with pine needles.

Soon the trail joins an old narrow grassy road and makes a ninety-degree turn to the left. After only a few steps, you can hear the din of the Ottauquechee coursing through the gorge. After another 100 yards the road emerges from the woods onto an even wider dirt road paralleling the gorge.

Directly across this road you can pause at an overlook. Here the Ottauquechee is dwarfed by the sides of the chasm stretching high above. After viewing the gorge from this vantage point, return to the road and go left up the hill. At the .7-mile mark you begin a long climb to the US 4 bridge.

Cresting the hill, with the bridge in sight ahead, note the blue trail marker leading sharply into the woods on the right. This will be your return route. Continue straight, however, for a look at the gorge from the top. You pass under the bridge and almost immediately climb at a reverse forty-five-degree angle (right) up to US 4.

Peering into the gorge on the north side can give you a dizzy feeling. Hemlock, pine, and maple grip the sides of this jagged slashway and funnel your gaze downward. The Ottauquechee River courses lavalike along the bottom of this deep cleft. Stretches of fast water scratch the dark surface with white.

Cross the bridge to the other side. The gorge appears much straighter and narrower here. The river moves faster and has molded deep impressions into the rocks.

Retrace your steps on US 4, around

the gift shop, and back down under the bridge. Watch for the blue marker on your left.

The return trail eases back into the deeper woods and meanders parallel to and below US 4. The quiet softness of the forest is shattered intermittently by the droning of automobiles.

You pass over a small stream with assistance from fallen logs and immediately turn right past a massive dead, barkless tree. Follow the path beside the water.

Two hundred yards after crossing the brook the trail runs into a wider path at a ninety-degree angle. Follow the blue markers and the arrow pointing left. The path bears gradually around to the right and unexpectedly leads onto a narrower way at a forty five-degree angle. Go right here. Be alert; it is easy to miss this turn.

The trail becomes quite steep as it climbs up to the circular park road at campsite #15. Go left past the rest rooms and Quechee State Park bulletin board. You may now either continue a short distance along the road or take the little path straight across the open field to your car.

23

Mount Tom

Class: II
Distance (round trip): 2.4 miles
Hiking time: 1 1/2 hours
Vertical rise: 640 feet
USGS 7.5' Woodstock North

Traditionally, when the citizenry of Woodstock become concerned about some aspect of their town, action is sure to follow. Concern that the town's natural setting might be lost through development has led to the creation of three public parks inside the town's limits. Two of these, Billings Park on Mount Tom on the north side of town, and Mount Peg, just south of the village, are on tracts that were donated outright to the town. The Woodstock Park Commission is responsible for overseeing these two properties. The third, Faulkner Park, also on the north side of town and adjacent to Billings, is open to the public but is owned and managed by the trustees of the Faulkner estate.

This loop hike from the village to the two peaks of Mount Tom uses the trail system of Billings Park, with the exception of one small segment of the Faulkner Trail, which a spur links with one of the Billings Park trails. Billings Park was given to the town in 1953 in the memory of Mary M. Billings French by her children. It has been left in its natural state except for the areas immediately next to the trails and a small plot around a Girl Scout cabin. The 155-acre tract extends from River Street,

on the north side of the Ottauquechee River, up the rugged, rocky south slope of Mount Tom, and north across the summit area. There are some magnificent views from the two peaks.

To reach the start of this hike from the village green in the center of Woodstock on US 4, walk or drive through the Union Street covered bridge and turn right onto River Street. The trail begins just past the River Street cemetery, on the left a short distance from the bridge.

The trail starts as a gently sloping, winding bridle path. Within .3 mile you come to the Girl Scout cabin on your left. Just beyond it the trail to the summit of Mount Tom angles sharply to the left.

You will not have been long on this trail when you reach the first of two Link Trails to the Faulkner Trail. Bear right at this junction and continue to the next, which is .2 mile from the cabin. The uppermost route on your left here is the Link Trail that you will use on your return.

Again bearing right, you climb across the slope of Mount Tom. Just beyond a sharp switchback, you meet the North Peak Trail, which angles off to the right.

You have now traveled .6 mile from River Street. The rocky bluff of Mount Tom stretches upward directly before you.

Bear right onto the North Peak Trail, which is about .5 mile long. The way leads at first steeply and then more gradually up the shoulder of Mount Tom. After a sharp turn to the left, the North Peak trail passes the Back Loop Trail and continues to the summit itself. The North Peak of Mount Tom is 1,320 feet above sea level and roughly 640 feet higher than the village. There are views from here south and west.

Continuing left on the North Peak, the trail ends where it intersects an old carriage road that leads to Mount Tom's South Peak.

Bear left and follow the old road .3 mile as it dips down and then up to the South Peak. Although this peak is the lower of the two (1,240 feet), the views are more impressive. Below, the Ottauquechee River winds through the village of Woodstock and the green fields of farms to the east.

Your route from here back into the valley is by way of the Faulkner Trail. Well-defined, it cuts steeply down the face of Mount Tom for less than .1 mile before taking a zigzagging course that lessens the gradient considerably. In .4 mile you will reach the upper Link Trail, on your left. It leads in .2 mile back to the trail to the Girl Scout cabin. Take it to retrace your steps or continue down the Faulkner Trail to Mountain Avenue. Turn left on this street, which leads directly to Union Street and the covered bridge.

24

Amity Pond Natural Area

Class II
Distance (round-trip): 2.6 miles
Hiking time: 1 3/4 hours
Vertical rise: 660 feet
USGS 7.5' Woodstock North

In 1969 Elizabeth and Richard Brett deeded this land to the state of Vermont to be used for hiking, snowshoeing, cross-country skiing, and horseback riding. No motor vehicles are allowed here. Even radios are prohibited. The Amity Pond Natural Area is a place to refresh your senses and spirit.

Fires are permitted only at the shelters. Hikers are asked to remain on the trails to avoid any possible damage to the area. Picking or cutting flowers, plants, or trees is also not allowed.

From Woodstock drive north on VT 12 for 1.2 miles. As the road forks, bear right toward South Pomfret. Stay on this road for 2 miles to another fork at the South Pomfret Post Office. Go right toward Pomfret. Drive for 4.7 miles and then go left onto the paved road just after the wide bend to the right. After .3 mile turn left at another fork onto a dirt road. Drive 2.2 miles and look for the entrance to the Amity Pond Natural Area.

The absence of large signs is in keeping with the area's philosophy. Watch carefully for the blue and orange diamond-shaped trail markers and a poster sign on a tree to the left of the road. There is limited parking across the road from the entrance. Pass through the narrow opening in the barbed-wire fence into a field dotted with young red pine. Almost immediately after the trail begins, a short spur leads left to the rustic Amity Pond Shelter built in 1969. The shelter faces a temporary pond, which is part of a water conservation experiment.

Return to the main trail and follow its wide, flat grassy path. The blue and orange diamonds guide you along.

To the right of the height-of-land is Amity Pond itself, bounded by a small area of ledge, shrubs, tall grass, and reeds. You can look to the south from here and see the saddle-backed hump of Mount Ascutney. The view to the west takes in the high pointed top of Killington Peak and the cone-shaped summit of Pico Peak.

An interesting tale describes how the pond got its name. Two girls who attended the East Barnard school together became chums and promised each other "friendship forever." When one married a man from the town of Pomfret and the other wed a man from Barnard, it was difficult for them to get together. So, by mail, they arranged to share a basket lunch on specified days at the grassy hill beside this tiny pond, which thus became known as Amity Pond.

The wide, flat trail winds down through the large, open meadow. Tall grasses, goldenrod, and milkweed brush your legs. Keep to the far right of the field—you will see an opening in the trees and a blue tin can top for a blaze. Passing between sections of an old stone wall, the trail enters the hardwood forest. Wide, flat and easy to walk, the trail bends to the right and meanders gradually down through the woods. After .6 mile you enter a small meadow where a spur leads left to the Sugar Arch Shelter.

Now grassy, the way passes beneath power lines and continues steadily downward. Thick stands of hemlock and occasional pines and spruces line the trail and a small brook parallels it to the left.

Just short of the 1-mile mark you step out into a huge open field. To the right are a church and cemetery; to the left, a farm house. Make your way across the open area to the road straight ahead.

Turn left onto the road and walk past a second farmhouse on the left. Just beyond, you cross the cement-sided road bridge over Broad Brook. Approximately 60 feet beyond the bridge the trail leads left off the road. It drops down through shrubbery to a trail sign and the brook.

Be alert for animal signs along the water and in damp areas ahead. A raccoon's imprint is particularly distinctive.

Amity Pond

Its front and hind feet have a pad with five slender toes. The tracks are usually paired with the left hind foot placed beside the right fore foot.

Rock hop across Broad Brook and continue up into the woods (ignore the short spur to the left just after the brook). Evergreens canopy the trail as the orange and blue markers lead you beside the brook for a short distance. Swing left and climb the moderate grade beside a barbed-wire fence. After a series of upward twists and turns, the path crosses a small stream via slim, cut logs.

After 2 miles a trail joins from the left. Continue straight here. A stone wall parallels the route as you climb steadily upward. The path flattens out and passes beneath power lines. It then drops down a moderate grade to the bottom of a narrow gully and crosses over a trickling brook at 2.2 miles.

Beyond the brook you ascend a steep incline to the right. Near the top of this open-wooded slope you enter a small, round clearing. The trail swings sharply left and climbs to the top of a hill lined by a sparkling stand of white birches.

Cresting this rise, you step out into the southwestern corner of the meadow where Amity Pond is located. Follow the orange and blue markers to the trail junction just below the height-of-land beside Amity Pond. Continue past the pond and follow the path back to your car.

Slack Hill

Class: II
Distance (round trip): 3.1 miles
Hiking time: 1 3/4 hours
Vertical rise: 542 feet
USGS 7.5' Plymouth

The leisurely woods walk to Slack Hill's summit takes you through the 3,400-acre Pinney Hollow area of the rambling Calvin Coolidge State Forest, which covers 12,000 acres and is divided into several separate parcels. Whether you're camping at the park or are here for the hike only, you'll enjoy the wide trails, gradual slopes, and open wooded area. Allow plenty of time for an unhurried, relaxing, and beautiful walk.

From Bridgewater Corners drive south 4.2 miles on VT 100A to the entrance of the Calvin Coolidge State Forest. (Plymouth, the tiny community where Calvin Coolidge was born, is 2 miles further south. The Coolidge Homestead is open to the public.)

Follow the long, winding road from the park entrance to the Contact Station (admission and information booth). Pay the 50¢ per-person charge for day use of the facilities and park in the area to the right. If you are taking dogs along for the walk, remember to bring their leashes, as Vermont State parks do not allow dogs to run loose.

The blue-blazed trail begins behind and to the right of the booth. A longer trail (see map) begins back nearer the entrance of the park. However, it is used primarily as a pulp road—timber is harvested to insure proper management of trees and other vegetation—and does not have the scenic appeal of the footpath.

Your route is divided into three separate sections. The gradual climb to the top of Slack Hill is 1.3 miles long. A descent of .9 mile brings you to the parking lot at the picnic area. Another downhill walk of just under 1 mile along the road connecting the picnic area with the Contact Station will return you to your car.

The wide packed-dirt trail leads gradually upward through thin young trees. Occasional clumps of fern and slender striped maple provide the only major ground cover between the tree trunks. After topping the incline, the path levels and begins a series of short dips and rises. The trail becomes so wide open that it is possible to wander off the path. Keep an eye on the frequent blue blazes.

After .5 mile an arrow points to the right for a short trail back to the Contact Station and woodshed. Follow the blue blazes sharply left here. This area supports a wide variety of animal life. You might be lucky enough to see any of the following: chipmunks, red squirrels, partridge, woodcock, deer, or rabbits. Songbirds also flourish, particularly the inquisitive chickadee. To attract the black-capped chickadees try kissing the back of your hand or whistling chick-a-dee-dee-dee.

The trail begins to slab gradually across the hillside. It continues to pass through typical hardwood forests, which have only a scattering of the elms that were once prominent in them. The American elm seeds are eaten by grouse, squirrels, and opossum. Deer and cottontail rabbits browse the twigs. Unfortunately, this familiar tree is rapidly succumbing to Dutch elm disease.

After passing between thick stands of white birch, the path drops through a wide open area and joins a spur trail from the left. A sign here points left to Blueberry Lean-to. Swing sharply right.

Unusual clumps of maidenhair fern appear to the right of the trail. The finely divided leaves are four to sixteen inches wide and shaped like horseshoes. Individual leaves look like feathers in an Indian headdress as they waver in the slightest breeze.

Along the trail

The trail winds across the hillside and at the 1-mile point steps over an old stone wall. It becomes narrower and climbs toward the summit. Thick stands of red spruce and carpets of wavy broom moss flank the path.

The ground levels as you come to the summit. A brown sign marks the spot. There are no views from here but you enjoy a peaceful relaxed feeling as you meander through evergreens.

Follow the blue blazes past the elevation sign and descend gradually .9 mile to the picnic area. Single logs imbedded diagonally in the dirt occasionally cross the trail. This is a system of erosion prevention that directs rain and snow runoff to the sides of the trail and keeps the flat path in fine condition.

Nearing the picnic area the trail switches back to the right. It winds between a thick area of white birches and red spruces. Glimpses of parked autos through towering white pines signal the end of the woodland trail. When you reach the paved park road, go right and follow it .9 mile to your car.

26

Shrewsbury Peak

Class: II
Distance (round trip): 3.6 miles
Hiking time: 2 1/2 hours
Vertical rise: 1,757 feet
USGS 7.5' Killington Peak

You leave the clutches of civilization
before beginning this hike. No horns or
screeching tires pierce the quiet as you
start the roller-coaster-like climb to
Shrewsbury Peak. With each step the
quiet of the forest grows deeper.
Evergreen tunnels diminish thoughts of
the world you left behind. Silent mountains await your company at the summit.

Take VT 100 from either West
Bridgewater or Plymouth Union to the
dirt road leading west, .2 mile south of
the tip of Woodward Reservoir. This road
can be recognized by its exceptionally
wide entrance beside the brown post
and wire guard rails of VT 100. Follow it
3.3 miles to the short dirt road that leads
to the log shelter at the former Northam
Picnic Area. (Just before reaching this
turn there will be a narrow dirt road on
the right. Go past it and take the next
right.) Park in the area in front of the
shelter. The blue-blazed trail begins
behind and to the left of the shelter.

Before you've gone very far, you'll
notice the unusual trees beside the trail.
Their dense conical shapes reach
almost to the ground. Scalelike leaves
one-eighth of an inch long or less hug
the twigs and branchlets of the flattened
sprays. The bark is very fibrous, with

many cross ridges. This tree—the northern white cedar—is a stranger to most of the hiking trails in this book. The northern white cedar grows in limestone soils and swamps, where it provides a favorite winter yarding food for deer. Moose, snowshoe hares, and cottontail rabbits also eat the twigs and foliage. Songbirds and red squirrels devour the seeds.

The trail swings around an old well. This water is not safe to drink. A sign here indicates you are 1.8 miles from Shrewsbury Peak.

Follow the moderate slope upward to the left. At .2 mile you reach a log lean-to with a bunk area tucked up under its short front overhang. A stone fireplace highlights this cozy, primitive dwelling. There is also an outhouse.

The path continues gradually to the top of Russell Hill, elevation 2,540 feet. It levels out and then descends a gentle slope past moss-covered glacial boulders.

At .4 mile you look down into a ravine and then begin the steep descent to its bottom. Once there, the only way is up as you follow the blue blazes over the boulder-strewn hillside. After cresting the ravine slope the trail becomes more gradual. It leads over, around, and between a long series of rocks and boulders. Many are covered with wavy brown moss.

The path crosses an old grassed-in road. It makes a short climb and then levels out for a short distance through beech trees and more boulders. After winding steadily but moderately upward, the path flattens out once again. For a surprisingly long way, it meanders over rock-and-root-free ground. Then, a long sloping upward climb reminds you that you are still heading for Shrewsbury Peak. Yellow birches appear to the left. Less striking than their white cousins, these trees have a creamy yellow or silver grey bark that peels in thin curls. Broken twigs give off a wintergreen odor.

You cross a dry brook bed at 1.3 miles (it will have water after a heavy rain). A small cairn points the way as the trail bears right and begins a steeper climb.

Thick, low balsams and red spruces begin to line the trail amid towering white birches. The balsam has long, flat, bright-green needles with two parallel silver stripes underneath. The red spruce has shorter needles that spiral closely around hairy twigs.

At approximately 1.4 miles you begin to see red blazes on some trees to the left of the trail. These denote the boundaries of the Calvin Coolidge State Forest, through which this part of the Shrewsbury Trail now travels. The double blue blazes on occasional trees indicate a sharp turn.

The path now becomes more cluttered with roots and rocks. It twists and turns through evergreen fragrance and becoming steeper, begins its final ascent to the summit.

Thick evergreens brush your body as you climb up over larger rocks and moss-covered ledge. Winding up through a long evergreen tunnel, you pass two overlooks on the right with views to the south.

The 3,720-foot summit is a small, ledged clearing with a wide view to the south and east. Blue arrows on the rock point in two directions. (The trail can be followed for another 2 miles to a junction with the Long Trail.)

Looking straight ahead (southeast) from the ledge you see the two-pronged summit of Mount Ascutney beyond the second ridge. New Hampshire mountains form the horizon. Just left (east) of Mount Ascutney is Mount Kearsarge, elevation 2,937 feet. Far to the right of Ascutney (south-southeast) is Monadnock Mountain, elevation 3,165 feet. Swinging in a chain to the south are closer Vermont mountains. Smith Peak and Ingalls Hill lead up to dual-peaked Burnt Mountain. Beyond are Bear and Salt Ash mountains. This splendid panorama is a marvelous backdrop to a picnic lunch.

Your return trip follows the same route back to your car.

Snow-dusted route to Shrewsbury Peak

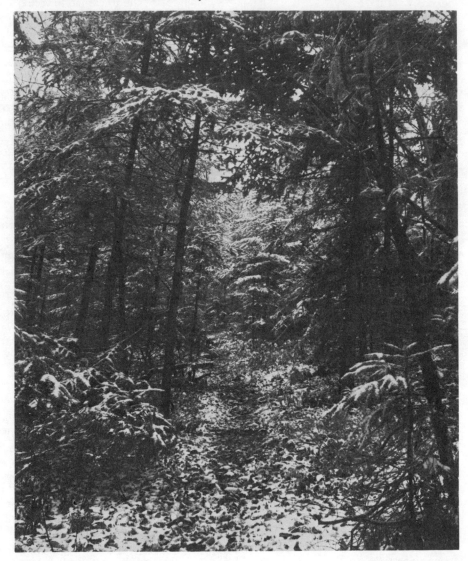

27

Killington Peak

Class: III
Distance (round trip): 6.8 miles
Hiking time: 4 1/4 hours
Vertical rise: 2,531 feet
USGS 7.5' Killington Peak, USGS 7.5' Rutland

At 4,241 feet, Killington is the second highest mountain in Vermont (only Mount Mansfield rises higher), and it is certainly one of the most popular. It's a four-season peak, with teeming ski slopes in winter and lots of good hiking the rest of the year. And always (weather permitting), the views are magnificent.

There are several ways to reach the top. For those who desire comfort, the gondola and main chairlift reach to within a short walk of the summit. But if you're more athletically inclined, the Bucklin Trail offers a nice combination of flat walking on old logging roads and steeper, more strenuous climbing over rocks. The 6.8-mile round trip is long enough for a challenge, yet short enough to allow plenty of time atop the mountain.

The trail begins at Brewers Corners on the Wheelerville Road. After you pass through Mendon on US 4 going east, take the first right (beyond a cement road bridge) onto the green-signed Wheelerville Road. Follow it exactly 4 miles to a sharp bend to the right. This is Brewers Corners. The trail begins on the left just before the bend. The blue blazes and sign are just in off the road.

Following an old logging road, you pass beneath towering pines, balsams, and spruces. The roar of water can be heard to the left as you leave the conifers and enter the hardwood forest.

Shortly you come to Brewers Brook. Cross it via the heavy wooden bridge that lists sharply to the right. The road begins a very gradual climb but continues to be easy to walk. The woods thin out as the hillsides slope upward above you to the right.

At .8 mile the road stops where two branches of the brook meet. Cross to the middle grassy area and then follow the brook up to the left. Step carefully along this very rocky section. About .2 mile farther along, the path meets slow-flowing water and crosses over it. Blue blazes mark the way to the continuation of the logging road on the other side.

Now on the north side of the brook, you quickly cross one of its small tributaries. The grade begins to increase slightly as goldenrod closes in from the sides. At approximately 1.7 miles red markers cross the trail and stretch into the woods on both sides. These are the boundary markers for the Calvin Coolidge State Forest. Just beyond, the trail forks and the blue blazes lead you to the right.

The pleasantly flat logging road now gives way to moderate slopes strewn with loose rocks. The trail narrows and winds upward through thin trees. Occasional openings to the left enable you to see towering companion peaks.

Winding upward to the right, the path becomes much greener along the edges. Hay-scented ferns swarm over the ground. Broom moss, wood sorrel, and shining club moss cluster around the bases of trees.

At approximately 2.3 miles the trail crosses an old grassed-in logging road and continues upward through white birches which are quickly replaced by evergreens. The path flattens out a bit before swinging upward again to the right through thick stands of conifers. Note that you have just left the north side of the ridge and are now climbing straight up the slope in a southerly direction.

Red osier dogwood brushes against your legs and fills a large clearing to the left. This shrub is common throughout northern New England. Its branches spread loosely along the ground and rise no higher than six feet at the tips. The leaves are prominently veined, nearly smooth underneath, and pale. It bears dark red branches in winter and small white flowers in flat-topped clusters in June.

At 3.2 miles you reach an intersection and go left toward (clearly visible) Cooper Lodge. The trail winds sharply right just before the lodge and joins the Long Trail South for approximately 100 feet as far as a clearing. The Long Trail bears right here, and you continue straight ahead up the .2-mile spur to Killington Peak.

Rocks and small boulders fill the blue-blazed trail as it veers right at a fork. A tumble of rocks and ledge makes the climbing more difficult. Hands become as useful as feet here. Passing upward through scrub growth, you reach the open-ledged summit.

The mountaintop is surprisingly, and disappointingly, civilized. A lookout tower

*View of Killington's
summit, with
Pico Peak beyond*

and radio installation greet you first. On a short spur trail to the east is the Killington Gondola Terminal and Restaurant

(In 1763 Rev. Sam Peters, a Connecticut clergyman, rode through central Vermont on a preaching and baptizing mission. He claimed to have christened the state ''Verd-Mont,'' from the summit of Killington.)

From various points you can see to the distant horizons in all directions. Pico Peak rises to the immediate north.

Green Mountain peaks are visible north to Mount Mansfield and south to Glastenbury Mountain. The city of Rutland nestles in a long valley to the west, and beyond are the Taconics, Lake Champlain, and the Adirondacks. Eastward are the White Mountains, while Mount Ascutney is the only prominent peak to the southeast.

When ready, return to your car via the same trail.

28

Deer Leap Mountain

Class: II & V
Distance (round trip): 2.7 miles
Hiking time: 2 hours
Vertical rise: 680 feet
USGS 7.5' Pico Peak

This climb could be viewed as two separate hikes. The loop you'll make will bring you to Deer Leap Mountain's two peaks and across its saddle over vastly different routes. The ascent via the Long Trail and Deer Leap Trail is gradual-to-moderate; the descent from Little Deer Leap (the southern peak) is precipitous. You'll use your hands often as you pick your way down over steep-ledged sections.

Start at the Long Trail North in Sherburne Pass. At the height-of-land on US 4 between Rutland and Sherburne you will see the Long Trail Lodge. Just to the east a sign marks the Long and Appalachian trails. There is off-the-road parking on both sides of the highway here.

Climb 150 feet from the road to the fork where the Deer Leap and Long trails split. You are taking the gradual way up and the steeper way down. Keep right on the white-blazed Long Trail.

The trail winds along the mountainside. Above and to the left hundreds of large boulders crowd the slope. The path is also littered with rocks and small boulders, so walk carefully. Below to the right US 4 parallels your route. The loud motor vehicle noises remind you that you haven't yet escaped civilization.

The trail swings upward to the left and begins to slice along the east side of the slope. Huge masses of ledge jut out from the hillside above, and eventually the path comes up to meet them. Pass upward through a slender opening between these giants. Roots and stones continue to make the walking rough as you climb the moderate grade. Then, as you meander over short dips and rises, the slope becomes more gradual and the footing smoother.

After roughly .5 mile the woods suddenly open before you. The sloping hillsides disappear and you enter a flat clearing. Many signs mark this important trail intersection. This is the junction of the Appalachian and Long trails. From here the Long Trail continues north to Canada, while the Appalachian swings east toward New Hampshire and its northern terminus on Mount Katahdin in Maine. Keep left on the Long Trail.

The path remains flat except for occasional bends around boulders. Becoming strewn with rocks, it swings gradually up to the left. It passes a huge moss-covered boulder supporting an old birch tree. Roots cling to the stone surface like octopus tentacles.

Thin, fragile-looking trees line the trail as it begins a very gradual, long, winding descent. At 1.2 miles the Deer Leap and Long trails rejoin. Follow the blue-blazed Deer Leap Trail as it turns sharply left.

Short spruces take over the left hillside as the trail passes briefly through a steeper section. The grade becomes more gradual as you wind through more young spruces, and then more moderate, and finally steep, before returning to its familiar gradual incline.

Some of the large tree trunks and stumps that line the way have hundreds of small, evenly spaced holes girdling their bark. They were made by the yellow-bellied sapsucker. This bird makes the holes while eating the inner bark. He wisely returns later to eat both the sap and the insects that have been attracted to it.

Thick stands of spruce gather around the trail just before it passes through an area dense with ferns. Two large trees next to a huge boulder on the right mark a lookoff. Limited views to the northwest are available here.

The path winds upward and becomes steeper. It flattens out in an open area edged by ledge on the left. Passing through thick spruces, the path becomes spongy with needles. You soon reach a sign titled Deer Leap Height (just west of Big Deer Leap, the northern peak of Deer Leap Mountain). The elevation here is 2,770 feet.

The trail drops first moderately, then gradually, into the valley separating Deer Leap Mountain's two peaks. At 2.2 miles you come to a sign indicating it is about .5 mile to Sherburne Pass.

Cross a small brook and climb steeply through white birches and under overhanging ledge. Walk along the ridge to the sign for Little Deer Leap, the southern peak. The elevation here is 2,580 feet.

The path twists and turns through a

Lower lookout on Deer Leap Mountain

spruce-lined area. Traffic sounds get louder as you begin to descend. Soon you reach a huge mass of white, quartz-streaked ledge. This is the Upper Lookout. Climb up for striking views of Sherburne Pass and surrounding mountains. One hundred feet below, you walk out onto the Lower Lookout. From this ledge you look up to Pico Peak across Sherburne Pass and down to US 4.

The remaining descent to your car is very steep and slippery. You slide down over smooth ledge and through jumbled sections of massive boulders. After stepping down a log ladder and using a nylon cable along a particularly steep section, you drop quickly to US 4 and your car.

29

Blue Ridge Mountain

Class: III
Distance (round trip): 4.8 miles
Hiking time: 2 1/2 hours
Vertical rise: 1,487 feet
USGS 7.5' Chittenden

A beautiful, cascading waterfall and hordes of yellow birches enrich the sides of the 2.4-mile-long trail up the south side of Blue Ridge Mountain. It takes you to the mountain's summit after a steep ascent through deciduous forests and a final meandering walk through evergreens. Once there, you get one of the best close views of the Coolidge Range. You can also look to the west beyond Rutland to Bird and Herrick mountains with the Adirondacks on the horizon. On a clear day when the light is right, you can see what appears to be a misty field just in front of the Adirondacks. This, of course, is Lake Champlain. Stratton and Dorset mountains lie to the south and southwest.

To reach the trail's start, drive east on US 4 for 6.2 miles from the junction of US 4 and US 7 in Rutland. Turn north onto Old Turnpike Road (the sign reads simply "Turnpike Road"). Drive .6 mile and turn left onto the second dirt road, where there is an arrowed sign to the Tall Timber Camping Area (a private campground). There are also trail signs for "Blue Ridge." Bear left at the fork and continue until you come to the large

main building. Park your car in the field to the left.

Following the road, walk to the right beyond this large brown building. Continue right at the fork here. You will quickly come to a number of signs. An arrow points the way to Blue Ridge. The trail you want is marked with tin can tops painted blue.

Turn left into the woods and follow the blue blazes, which are initially paired with the green ones of the shorter Green Trail. A trail junction soon appears. Your route leaves the Green Trail, crosses the brook, and bears right. Very soon, you ford the brook again and resume a gradual walk.

The sides of the path are thickly forested with evergreens. After paralleling the brook, you cross it once more at .3 mile, this time with the help of a log bridge. There is still no noticeable gain in elevation as the path proceeds over a series of dips and rises. After crossing still another stream, you follow an old road for a short distance.

There is one more stream to cross at .6 mile before the trail begins the more serious climb toward the summit. As-

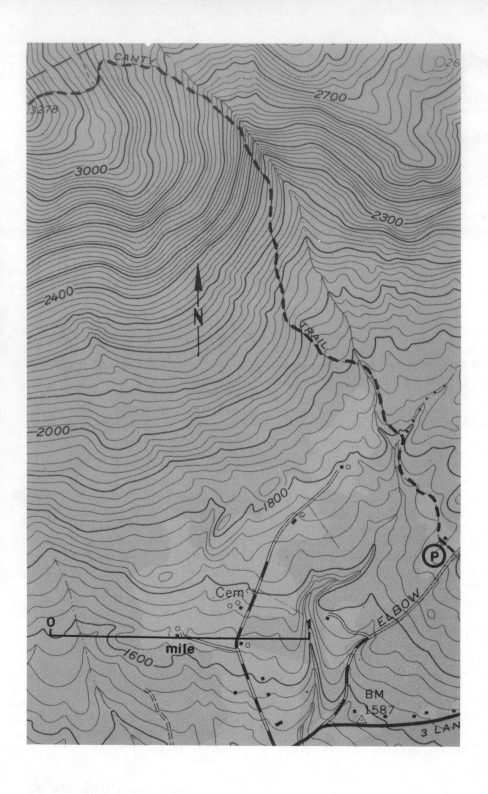

cend the steep stream bank and follow the winding path. It turns right onto another old road that parallels the brook below to the right.

The trail soon becomes more jumbled with rocks as the slope increases sharply. This is the steepest and most rugged section of the entire trail. Closer to the summit the path resumes its gradual, meandering ways.

There are large-tooth aspen along the pathside here. These northeastern trees resemble the trembling aspen somewhat, but have heavier twigs and larger, coarser leaves. The round-toothed, heart-shaped leaves are their most distinctive characteristic. The soft, light wood is used for pulp, excelsior, boxes, and matches.

After approximately 1.5 miles, you can hear rushing water below to the right. You might want to make your way down through the woods for a closer look. The cascading white water slides over smooth ledge and narrows to slither around rock outcroppings. It swirls into tranquil pools before tumbling downward again.

Paralleling the water, the path follows an old washed-out road. The higher sides offer more solid footing than the rutted, rocky middle. Yellow birches have been the most prominent tree along the way. These trees display silver-yellow bark and may grow as high as one hundred feet. Their double-toothed oval leaves have a wintergreen fragrance. Stands of these trees are a sign of rich, well-drained soil.

Continuing upward, the path becomes much more gradual. Shining club moss gathers its glossy spires to form sparkling green patches at the base of tree trunks. Evergreen spills cushion your walking as the trail brushes between spruces and balsams. The deliciously pungent fragrance of balsam fills your nostrils.

Cascade

After meandering upward to the left, the path suddenly swings right at 2.3 miles. Scramble over some ledge and enter the clearing at the summit. Above to the right are large rocks that serve as vantage points. They will enable you to see in all possible directions.

Return to your car by the same route.

30

Mount Carmel

Class: III
Distance (round trip): 4.4 miles
Hiking time: 2 1/2 hours
Vertical rise: 1,598 feet
USGS 7.5' Chittenden; USGS 7.5' Mount Carmel

The hike to the summit of Mount Carmel is a good one to save for an overcast day. The views from the top are limited in any event (the tower that used to offer a glorious panorama is down), and the forest is sufficiently varied to be of interest.

The first part of this hike follows the New Boston Trail. To reach its beginning, drive north on Mountain Top Road from the military memorial statue in the town of Chittenden. After 1.7 miles bear right onto the gravel road at the fork just beyond the Mountain Top Inn. This extremely rough road continues 1.4 miles to a brown and white sign on the left marking the start of the New Boston Trail. It will be the second sign you see for the New Boston Trail. Park well off the road here.

For the first 1.5 miles the blue blazes of this path follow a jeep trail. Much of this section is a pleasant walk, with only slight increases in elevation. The most rugged hiking and the most rapid rise in elevation occur during the final .3 mile to the summit.

Along the trail

The trail begins by entering the woods, passing between and beneath spirelike spruces. There are many logging roads so be careful to watch for the blue blazes marking the trail. After approximately .2 mile the road forks. Bear left here.

The pitch increases as you reach a second fork shortly ahead. Take the right road here. On both sides of the trail, rotting oak and beech stumps display bracketed growths of artist's fungus (so named for the pictures craftsmen like to paint on their smooth white undersides). Shades of brown and tan color the smoothly rippled sections of their upper surfaces.

Easy walking through beech-filled forests brings you to the third fork after .7 mile. Follow the blue blazes to the left here. After more gentle dips and rises you step over a small stream.

The red blazes of the Mount Carmel State Forest cross the path at 1.4 miles. Just beyond at the end of the jeep trail is the David Logan Shelter, used by hikers on the Long Trail, which is just ahead. A spring bubbles a bit north on the New Boston Trail.

Follow the winding, blue-blazed footpath to the left of the shelter. The packed-dirt path swings upward to the right and reaches the Long Trail at 1.7 miles.

Turn left onto the Long Trail and follow its white blazes north. Climbing steadily you arrive at the Mount Carmel Trail at 1.9 miles. Go right onto this unblazed but well-trodden path.

The way swings around to the left through bunches of hobblebush. Its leaves are large (four-to-eight inches), nearly round, finely toothed, and heart-shaped at the base. In winter, distinctive buds will help you recognize this shrub: two small leaves enclose a tiny flower at the twig ends. These twigs and buds are favored by deer for winter browsing.

The path twists and turns up Mount Carmel's south slope. You really have to lean into this steep ascent. After entering a small clearing covered with spruce and balsam spills, the way climbs straight up to the summit.

You know you have reached the top when you find the former tower laying on its side. There are limited views to the west.

Follow the same route back to your car.

31

Abbey Pond

Class: II
Distance (round trip): 3.4 miles
Hiking time: 2 1/4 hours
Vertical rise: 1,250 feet
USGS 7.5' South Mountain

You will be touched by Abbey Pond's primitiveness and tranquility. An early morning or late afternoon visit to the pond might acquaint you with some of its more bashful neighbors. The masked nocturnal raccoon may leave his long-fingered pawprints after feeding on frogs and crayfish. Deer come to drink and browse on pondside shrubbery. Muskrats nest along the sides of the pond and sometimes build above-water homes like those of the beaver.

Drive north on US 7 into Middlebury. Pass the Addison County Court House and take the next right. At the stop sign bear right onto Seminary Street Extension. Bear left at the fork after 1.4 miles onto Quarry Road. Follow it to the end where it meets VT 116 (Case Street) and turn left (north). After another .7 mile you'll spot a sign for the Abbey Pond Trail on the east side of the road. Turn east onto the dirt road, which divides immediately. Take the right fork and follow the dark blue blazes on the trees.

Approximately .4 mile after turning onto the dirt road you'll reach an intersection. Straight ahead, blue blazes mark the start of the trail. Pull your car well

off the road to avoid interfering with gravel trucks.

Follow the blue blazes along an old logging road. The track is wide and gradual. Some rocks intrude but are easily avoided. Then giant glacial boulders, many with trees and mosses flourishing atop their great masses, appear to the right.

The pitch increases. Swinging left, the dirt path passes below moss-covered ledge. After approximately .2 mile you cross over fast-flowing Muddy Brook, which finds its source in Abbey Pond. To the right a twenty-five-foot waterfall spills into a series of small pools.

Soon the trail swings right and begins to parallel the brook, whose muffled rushing will accompany you for some time. At .6 mile the brook again passes beneath the trail. Bearing left, the path maintains a steady upward incline. The brook courses along the bottom of the ravine below.

At 1.1 miles, on a more gentle incline, the trail passes over a black boggy area and crosses a gentler section of the brook via narrow logs. Beyond the brook the path wanders over and around small rocks. It remains flat, with only minimal dips and rises, the rest of the way to the pond. The ground may be a bit spongy underfoot.

You come out of the thick woods, and arrive at Abbey Pond. Two small peaks rise above and are reflected in its waters. Looking around the pond you'll see a beaver dam at the near end. Look down the pond to the dead trees rising at the other end and you'll see the lodge itself.

Sit quietly on a sun-warmed rock near the water's edge; watch and listen. A salamander may be scuttling along the bottom. These tailed amphibians eat insects, worms, and other small invertebrates. In early summer, their eggs are found in jellylike clusters in the shallows.

The pond is a haven for ducks and geese. Abbey Pond's shallowness and its aquatic plants attract the surface-feeding ducks such as mallards and blacks. You may see them "tipping up" as they eat off the lush bottom.

The belted kingfisher also lives here. He has distinctive blue-grey markings, a white throat band, a large bill, and a crested head. He flies erratically yet can hover suspended over the water before plunging in for small fish.

The trout, too, find Abbey Pond beautiful. Creating circles of ripples as they surface for food, they often leap completely out of the water in their pursuit of insects.

Return to your car filled with some of the quiet of this woodland pond.

Abbey Pond

32

Mount Abraham

Class: III
Distance (round trip): 5 miles
Hiking time: 3 1/2 hours
Vertical rise: 1,642 feet
USGS 7.5' Lincoln

Mount Abraham is among the more popular climbs for day hikers, as well as a favorite with backpackers walking the Long Trail. Its easy access and striking views—it has one of the most far-reaching panoramas on the entire Long Trail—make it a very desirable destination.

Early settlers called Mount Abraham "Potatoe Hill" because of its resemblance to an oversized, well-banked potato mound. This name was not completely accepted, however, and map publishers changed it to Lincoln Mountain—for the Revolutionary War figure General Benjamin Lincoln. When Colonel Joseph Battell bought the mountain in the late 1800s (as part of his plan for conserving Vermont forests), he renamed it Mount Abraham, after our sixteenth president. He then named the neighboring mountain to the north Lincoln Peak.

To reach the stretch of the Long Trail that climbs Mount Abraham, travel along the Lincoln-Warren Highway from either Lincoln or Warren to the top of the Lincoln Gap. There is ample parking just below the crest, on the Warren side, both off and along the road. However, on a clear weekend you might arrive to find the roadside already packed with vehicles of all kinds.

Walk up the road, toward Lincoln, to the height-of-land, where you will find the trail ascending a short, steep embankment on the north side of the highway. At the top of the embankment the trail forks. Stay to the left. The path narrows as it passes behind slender young birches. White blazes guide you right and gradually upward. Surprisingly, there are a number of abrupt descents during the first half of your trek up Mount Abraham. The trail swings sharply left, then right, as it drops down over rooted steps. Dipping steadily, it switches back sharply right and winds past a long series of moss-covered ledges.

Then the smoothness of the path yields to rocks as you pass upward through snowy birches. A small section of ledge insures a gradual rise. Once on top you gaze down a short, steep dropoff. Serpentine roots cling to the ledge, providing sure footing. Moving gradually upward, you come to red blazes flanking and crossing the trail. These mark the boundary of the Green Mountain National Forest.

Two huge boulders squeeze the trail

at the 1.2-mile mark. (They are called ''the Carpenters'' after two trail workers so named.) Old stumps, rotted into a variety of poses, dot the way.

The 2,410-foot base elevation at Lincoln Gap is responsible for the fact that the highway through it is closed in winter and for the lack of traditional hardwood forests along this trail. Instead, the trailsides teem with fluffy young spruce and balsam. They are so closely packed that you wonder how they will survive. Stately older trees rise above these younger ones.

An opening in the thick trees suddenly appears. Straight ahead you can see the massive dome of Mount Abraham. Tree-covered except for the actual summit, it appears quite imposing from this distance. You are now roughly 1 mile from the top.

A trickling brook crosses the trail. It offers cool, refreshing water and a good excuse to rest. Just ahead, the Battell Trail joins from the left. Battell Shelter is 250 yards upward to the right. A sturdy, smooth-sided structure, it can sleep six to eight hikers. Spring water is available 100 feet to the east.

Nearing Mount Abraham's summit

From the shelter take the main trail to the left. Thick stands of spruce and balsam create a cloistered atmosphere. Twists and turns over intermittent stretches of ledge necessitate careful stepping. Approaching the summit amid dwarfed scrub growth, the trail confronts an unusually beautiful boulder. White but veined with black, the giant piece of quartz is surely a rarity. Against the drab grey-greens of the ledge and spruce, it stands out strikingly.

Reaching the summit, you see several circles of piled rocks. Looking like the bottom of unfinished stone igloos, these barriers offer protection from blustery winds. If you look closely on the ground, you will find the surveyor's disk with the words "Potatoe Hill" on it.

The views are superb. You can look west across Lake Champlain and clearly see the Adirondacks, with Mount Marcy most prominent. Southward, Green Mountain peaks stretch as far as Killington. Mount Ascutney looms on the horizon to the southeast. Mounts Lafayette and Washington are in the distant east. Looking north, you can follow a panoramic profile from the distinctive Camel's Hump, past Mount Mansfield, north to Jay Peak and Belvidere Mountain.

The Warren-Sugarbush Airport (a local center for soaring enthusiasts) is below and to the east. You can become mesmerized by the gliders if you're on Mount Abraham when the weather is clear and the winds are right.

Return to reality; your transportation awaits 2.5 miles below at Lincoln Gap.

33

Mount Ellen

Class: III
Distance (round trip): 9.7 miles
Hiking time: 6 1/2 - 7 hours
Vertical rise: 2,508 feet
USGS 7.5' Mount Ellen

Although Mount Ellen's wooded summit is the ultimate destination on this challenging hike, the best views are from just below the peak. The ascent itself is steep, rugged, and continuous.

Mount Ellen shares with Camel's Hump the honor of being Vermont's third highest peak. Only Killington and Mansfield rise higher. This mountain is not as close to access roads as the others, however, so the trails to its summit are longer. The climb is steady and though gradual at times has you leaning into the slope almost all the way. Prepare for a long day's hiking.

From the junction of VT 17 and VT 116 northeast of Bristol, go east on VT 17. Follow it 3.2 miles to the signed road leading to Jerusalem. Go right at the store and travel 1.2 miles to the wooden signpost at the corner of a road leading left. A small worn sign for the Jerusalem Trail will mark the beginning of your hike. Find a place here to park your car, being careful not to block the road or driveways.

Walk down the road for .7 mile. The start of the Jerusalem Trail is only a few hundred yards beyond the last house on your right. Follow the blue blazes into the woods and across a stream to the right.

Long, straight stretches, steady inclines, and slim trees characterize the surroundings over much of the first mile. At .8 mile, the path swings left and begins its steepest climb so far. A blue-blazed boulder, entrenched in the middle of the trail, marks the spot.

Thick stands of maples fill the forest as the grade maintains its upward trend. Both black and sugar maples grow here. (Black maple sap is also used to produce the famous Vermont maple syrup.) These two types of maples are distinguishable by their leaves. The black maple's are three-lobed with shallow notches and drooping edges. The sugar maple's are five-lobed with moderately deep notches and firm edges.

The trail bears right after 1.2 miles and changes direction from east to south. The high ridgeline of the Green Mountain chain now becomes visible above and to the left.

Dense thickets of hobblebush edge the path as it narrows and steepens. This straggly shrub is common throughout northern New England. The clustered five-petaled white flowers appear in May and June. The fruit (non-poisonous but acidic) begins to develop in August and changes from red to black at maturity.

The trail climbs a short, steep slope before weaving between stands of thin white birches. An old grassy road joins from the right at 1.7 miles. The way becomes refreshingly gradual in places, crosses two brooks, and then resumes its steep climb.

The easy walking has ended. For the next .5 mile the trail is very steep and rocks, ledge, and roots make the climbing more difficult.

At 2.3 miles the Jerusalem and Long trails meet. From here it is 1.8 miles to the summit of Mount Ellen. Turn right onto the Long Trail South. This section is quite typical of the Long Trail as it winds along ridges of the Green Mountains. It dips and rises while crossing from one side of the ridge line to the other. The footing ranges from rocky and rooty to boggy.

The rough trail descends gradually into a gully. Rising out, it passes through an area covered with many shades of green growth. Moss begins around tree trunks above the path and sweeps down over vertical ledge faces to the edge of the trail itself. Tree-filtered sunbeams highlight the rainbow of greenery.

Mount Ellen can be seen rising ahead as you continue through a lush, damp area. Rocks and dead logs are choked by a variety of plant life. Wood sorrel, wavy broom moss, and blister and reindeer lichen exist side by side.

At 3.1 miles the path climbs right over rocks and roots and begins a steady ascent to the summit. Dampness makes the trail slippery in spots.

A ski slope suddenly appears through

Trail to Mount Ellen

the trees. The trail comes out onto the cleared swath. Follow the slope up to the right along the edge of the woods, where there are white blazes and signs for the Long Trail. Continue to the upper station of the Sugarbush North chairlift. Look back down the slope for a view north to Camel's Hump and Mount Mansfield. Cross under the chairlift to the other side of the ski slope for a look to the east. Mount Alice and Bald and Scrag mountains are to the northeast. To the southeast you can pick out the peaks of Mount Cushman, Mount Olympus, and Rochester Mountain. New Hampshire summits form the distant backdrop.

Follow the white blazes past the end of the chairlift and up the short slope to the wooded summit. Find a spot in the sun to warm yourself and rest in preparation for the return trip.

34

Scrag Mountain

Class: III
Distance (round trip): 4.2 miles
Hiking time: 3 hours
Vertical rise: 1,491 feet
USGS 7.5' Waitsfield

The most beautiful white birch forests we've seen can be found in the cool woods on the slopes of Scrag Mountain.

To climb the trail through these handsome trees, drive to Waitsfield on VT 100. Turn southeast off VT 100 at the Jilson Public Library (the yellow brick building). Drive .4 mile, through a covered bridge, to a fork in the road. Follow the road to the left over a narrow bridge and up a steep hill for about .7 mile. Turn right onto a gravel road named Cross Road, which comes into a four-way intersection after .7 mile. Go straight across, and continue for still another .7 mile. At this point there is a small parking area on the left—the last available parking before the road becomes impassable for cars.

Walk up the grade .4 mile to a fork. A sign for the trail to Scrag Mountain points to the right. As you walk in this direction, your way is occasionally paralleled by low stone walls on either side. Further along, hemlocks form a natural boundary.

The way forks to both sides of a large hemlock .6 mile from the parking area. Follow the "Scrag Trail" sign to the left. The trail angles through dense patches

of ferns and into thicker woods. It is still a crude road at this point, quite bumpy and rocky.

A few minutes of walking bring you to a clear stream. This is the last certain water on the trail to the summit. Pause here to refresh and prepare yourself for the climb ahead. After the stream, the trail scrambles up over rocks, roots, and boulders. Young maples and beeches crowd the way. Though not excessively steep, the pitch of the upward grade is continually challenging.

An especially interesting large rock obstructs this lower part of the trail. Its surface is colored several shades of brown and pocketed with rounded depressions. Furry moss softens its face.

Scattered, solitary trees herald your approach to the promised assembly of white birches. They'll light your way for one-third of the hike to the summit. Pick your way across dried stream beds, by a decaying three-log bridge across a small gully, and then around the numerous rocks that have spilled down the trail. As you climb higher, spruces join, and finally replace, the white birches.

After 1.8 miles of hiking, the trail

divides. A sign indicates that the short trail straight ahead will lead to water at the first stream or the second well. However, it is better to carry your own drinking water to the top, as this supply is doubtful. Another sign points left toward Scrag Trail. Follow this left switchback .3 mile to the summit.

As you move along this section of the trail, look through the trees to the left for a glimpse of blue mountain silhouettes. The path winds over alternately rising and level areas as it swings widely right. Climb past a brown cabin into a small clearing. Limited views of various mountains, including the Lincoln Range, may be enjoyed from here.

For an opportunity to experience an extended circle of mountain views, continue along the trail to the top of Scrag Mountain (2,911 feet), where there used to be a fire lookout tower. Only four small pillars from the foundation remain. You'll climb over ledge on this last stretch of trail.

Camel's Hump and Mount Mansfield figure more prominently along the northwestern horizon. The Lincoln Range lines the west; south to north its peaks are: Mount Abraham, Lincoln Peak, Nancy Hanks Peak, Cutts Peak, and Mount Ellen. To the southwest you'll see the Presidential Range (not to be confused with the similarly named range in New Hampshire). Looking east you have: Butterfield, Spruce, and Signal mountains. Mount Hunger, Mount Worcester, and White Rock Mountain are to the north.

When ready, return by the same route.

35

Spruce Mountain

Class: III
Distance (round trip): 3.9 miles
Hiking time: 3 hours
Vertical rise: 1,177 feet
USGS 15' Plainfield; USGS 15' East Barre

Spruce Mountain lets you "get back to nature" in the purest sense. No summit roads or other encroachments of modern man scar its slopes. Its nearly twenty-five hundred-acres comprise one of the most remote mountain tracts remaining in the entire state.

The land also contains one of Vermont's best wildlife habitats. Black bear breed here, as do numerous other woodland creatures. One Spruce Mountain ornithological study a few years ago recorded sightings of seventy different kinds of birds.

The natural balance of Spruce Mountain has not yet been disturbed. But many of Vermont's unspoiled areas have been disappearing rapidly: sold to builders, developers, and speculators who care more for money than for the land. If we are to enjoy the peace, quiet, and exhileration of communing with nature, this area—and others like it—must remain "wild."

The road to the Spruce Mountain trail is located 4.2 miles south of Plainfield. Take the single road leading south from US 2 in the center of town and bear left at the first fork. Continue straight on this road to another fork. Go right here, following a sign to East Hill Road. Do not take the road to the left just after crossing a small bridge. Take the next left onto Spruce Mountain Road.

This road eventually swings left, with a narrow offshoot going right. Keep left here. Becoming very rocky and rutted, the road leads to an iron swing gate where there is ample parking on both sides. Should you be unable to reach this point by car, park at any of the widened areas along the way and walk the short distance to the gate. The red blazes to the right and left of the barrier mark the boundary of Jones State Forest.

The initial section of trail is a wide, smooth road. After about .5 mile the way forks to both sides of a large hemlock. Take the smaller trail to the left. As it crests a small knoll and begins heading downward, you can see the abandoned Spruce Mountain fire tower high in the distance to the left.

The way becomes increasingly grassy as it leads upward. The mountain's outline is occasionally visible through trees to the left as the road continues its gradual climb. When you swing left and enter dense woods, the grassy path fills with stones. Several damp, muddied patches lie ahead.

Cross-country ski trails have been cut through these woods and crisscross the main hiking trail ahead. They are marked with orange blazes. When you have a choice of paths to take, stay with the older trail. If you are uncertain, remember that the ski trails were cut because the main trail is too steep for skiers to use, but it is fine for hikers.

Making your way up this section of trail, stepping gingerly from rock to rock you come to a log bridge across a slow-moving brook. Beyond it the trail widens somewhat and becomes softer under-foot—although rocks continue to speckle the way. Walking is slower at times as you negotiate the bumpy footing.

Veering left, the path climbs moder-ately. Spruce and balsam line the trail as it continues to steepen. You approach two huge, looming glacial boulders at the 1.3-mile mark. Short spruces grow atop them and appear to be anchored by only a thick carpet of moss. The trail swings left in front of these gargantuan guards and begins a passage over slop-ing ledge.

Scraggy old spruces and balsams stand watch over smaller, bushy ones as the trail climbs more steeply. It seems impossible that the closely bunched young trees can find room to grow. The path passes over long sections of beautiful white-with-black-flecks granite ledge as it winds upward to the right.

View of Spruce Mountain

Then roots slither across the trail as it begins its final push to the top. The way suddenly levels out, becoming a dirt path lined with grass and ferns. The abbreviated height of the trees, combined with the low grass and shrubs at the trail sides, creates an open, airy atmosphere.

The old fire tower can be seen ahead, as you pass more slabs of granite. Both it and the small cabin just beyond, where the fire warden lived from April through October, are deserted and beginning to show signs of lack of maintenance. Planes now virtually monopolize surveillance duties in Vermont.

You can still climb to the top of the tower, but some of the wooden steps are starting to rot, so use care. The views from the tower are truly spectacular. On a clear day you can see west across Lake Champlain to the Adirondack peaks eighty miles away. Mount Washington's summit is visible seventy-five miles to the east. Numerous Vermont peaks can be seen within these perimeters.

Return to your car by the same route.

36

Osmore Pond and Little Deer Mountain

Class: II
Distance (round trip): 5.8 miles
Hiking time: 3 1/2 hours
Vertical rise: 660 feet
USGS 15' Plainfield

More than twenty thousand acres of land lie within the boundaries of Groton State Forest, making it the largest single unit of state-owned land in Vermont. Numerous game animals, especially deer, thrive here. Groton's spruce-fir swamps are a prime area for winter deer yarding.

People come to Groton State Forest for many reasons: they picnic, swim, camp, cook, hunt, go fishing and boating, enjoy the scenery, mob the refreshment stand, and, of course, go hiking. The trails marked with blue paint are for hikers and snowshoers only; those marked with orange reflecting diamonds are "multi-purpose" (all-terrain vehicles excluded). One hike here we like takes in both Osmore Pond and Little Deer Mountain. The walk to the pond is pleasantly undemanding; the hike up Little Deer, moderately strenuous.

Groton State Forest is located on the road that connects US 302 west of Groton and US 2 east of Marshfield. Drive from either end to the green and yellow sign for Groton State Forest listing Big Deer, Stillwater, and Lake Groton. Turn in here and follow the forest road for 1.6 miles to the new parking lot and nature center building, the first left past the Big Deer Campgrounds.

Walk back along the same road for .3 mile. On the right you will see brown and white signs for Osmore Pond and New Discovery. The path you are looking for starts into the woods just to the right of the signs. The blue blazes mark this as a trail for hikers only.

Sides of the trail overflow with fern growth. This gives the open woods a softly feathered look that accents the startling whiteness of paper birches and the shiny creaminess of yellow birches. The trail parallels a merrily flowing brook, occasionally dipping down near it. Where you begin to climb gradually the path swings away from the brook. Moving through the shadows of a stand of spruce, you can hear the wind brush the tree tops. Behind and below, the brook sound is soft and gushing.

At 1.2 miles you reach a small clearing where several trail signs are posted. A brown and white one points straight ahead for the Osmore Pond Hiking Loop. Heading in the direction the sign points, you shortly are able to see the waters of Osmore Pond. The loop trail winds gently around the edge of this lovely isolated pond. On the eastern side it parallels the shore about fifty feet in, but two foot-

paths lead to clear views at the water's edge. Rising above the southwestern end is Little Deer Mountain.

The sturdy log structures you pass are some of the more than twenty-five group camping lean-tos in the state forest. They may be used for wilderness camping according to the forest rules. In addition, state personnel maintain 225 individual camping sites.

You pass through occasional spruce bogs as you make your way around the pond. At the northern tip, the trail veers away from the water. You pick your way over another boggy area and a small streamlet. Continuing along the western shore, the path closely follows the pond's edge. Watch carefully for the blue-blazed markers as short young spruces and heavy side growth struggle to hide the trail. On this side you will also find a rustic picnic area with water and facilities.

From here you also have a clear view of Big Deer Mountain rising above the eastern shore of Osmore Pond. Nearby, sun-bleached logs poke their bulk above the water's surface. If you quietly approach one of these logs on a warm sunny day you may see pond sliders or other turtles basking in the sun.

View across Osmore Pond to Little Deer Mountain

Near the southern end of the pond, the trail winds gradually to the right, and power lines appear overhead. The path swings sharply left to a multi-signed trail junction.

Signs point straight ahead to Lake Groton, Peacham Pond, and Big Deer Mountain. Turn right here and follow the path beneath the power lines. After approximately 100 yards you will come to a sign pointing the way to Little Deer Mountain. It is .4 mile to the summit from here.

Go right on the blue-blazed path, which maintains a moderate pitch up the mountain. After a short distance, it makes a ninety-degree turn to the left. Watch carefully for the blue blazes at this point. The trail remains smooth and very enjoyable as it continues its moderate climb.

Near the summit the path swings left and leads into a small cleared area. There are limited views of nearby hills and an open look down the length of Lake Groton. To the southwest is Spruce Mountain, its high, pointed peak topped by an abandoned fire tower.

Hike back down the same trail to the sign for Little Deer Mountain. Go left onto the path beneath the power lines and back to the signed intersection. Go right toward Lake Groton, Big Deer Mountain, and Peacham Pond.

Bearing left, the path crosses a wood bridge. The brook beneath is the outlet of Osmore Pond. This is the start of the gurgling brook that parallels the stretch of trail you first walked.

A series of log planks have been placed on the trail to aid your passage over a final boggy area. Shortly after crossing this wet section you return to the junction of the Osmore Pond Hiking Loop, Big Deer Mountain Trail, and the trail to Lake Groton. You have now hiked 4 miles and have 1.2 miles left on the trail toward Lake Groton and the forest road and then .3 mile to the nature center parking lot.

37

Big Deer Mountain

Class II
Distance (round trip): 4.6 miles
Hiking time: 3 hours
Vertical rise: 912 feet
USGS 15' Plainfield

This hike offers you another nice way to spend your time in Groton State Forest (see Hike 36). Some entrances to trails are closed after Labor Day, but the one described here remains open.

Because the trail up Big Deer Mountain is both pretty and gentle all along its 2.3-mile length, it does not depend upon spectacular views for its charm. The flat, rolling path would be an ideal foliage walk in the fall. Maples, elms, and birches surround the occasional balsams and spruces. An openness along the trailsides inspires a sense of freedom and offers deep view into the woods.

The starting point for this hike is located in the parking lot for the new nature center at Groton State Forest. To reach it, drive along the road between US 302 west of Groton and US 2 east of Marshfield and turn in by the state forest sign for Lake Groton, Stillwater, and Big Deer Mountain. Follow the forest road 1.6 miles, past the Big Deer Campgrounds, to the nature center.

Walk to the far right-hand corner of the parking lot and pick up the Martins Pond Road-Peacham Bog Trail. In .5 mile you will find a sign for Coldwater Brook Trail. Turn left and stay on this trail for the rest of the hike.

Coldwater Brook

The path slithers around large rocks and passes through clusters of sparkling white birches as the hillside begins to slope steeply down to the right. The waters of Coldwater Brook can occasionally be seen and heard below. Rolling along over slight dips and rises, the trail veers left past a large triangular boulder. You cross several black muddy patches and then pass through stands of closely bunched spruces and balsams before re-entering the young hardwood forest.

Take time to observe the various kinds of greenery all around. Lady fern and pinulose woodfern swarm around hobblebush and striped maple. Close to the ground you can see shining club moss, bunchberries, and ground pine.

After passing two large glacial boulders guarding the sloping fields of fern to the left, the way narrows and becomes crisscrossed with roots. The trail swings right, and the hillside to the left draws closer. A gentle brook tumbles across the path at approximately .9 mile. Water caresses the many round mossy stones herded between its edges. Beyond the brook the trail swings sharply left before winding right toward Coldwater Brook.

The roar of gushing water draws your attention. Stop here for a delightful, shady respite. The brook's flowing softness turns frenzied as it rushes through a wide rocky chute. White water and foam gush into a quieter pool below. An archway in the wall of huge stones flanking the brook allows some water to flow to the edge, but most continues over a low dam into the placid pool.

Continuing up a moderate incline, you approach a fork in the trail. The Coldwater Brook Trail continues left here toward Osmore Pond. If you turn right you will cross the brook and within a few hundred yards find a winterized shelter. Retrace your steps and continue on the trail to Osmore Pond. It passes through light woods before crossing one of Coldwater Brook's small tributaries, which it then parallels awhile. Recrossing the brook, it begins a moderate climb to the right. Glacial boulders protrude from the open woods as the path becomes rockier. It leads over the rounded stones of an old stream bed before returning to

its flat, packed-dirt ways.

At 1.9 miles you enter a clearing with many signs. Follow the one to Big Deer Mountain up to the right. Climbing more steeply, you pass through expansive stands of white and then yellow birch. At 2.1 miles another sign points you sharply right. You are approximately .2 mile from the summit. Climbing through slender birches and over and around boulders, the trail becomes progressively steeper. Its edges are dotted with reindeer lichen, whose tiny antlered design makes them look like clumps of snowflakes on the ground.

The path finally leads onto an area of flat ledges surrounded by slim trees. You have a somewhat limited view through them to the northeast.

Your return from the summit will be by the same route.

38

Camel's Hump

Class: V
Distance (round trip): 8 miles
Hiking time: 6 - 6 1/2 hours
Vertical rise: 2,640 feet
USGS 7.5' Huntington; USGS 7.5' Waterbury

At 4,083 feet above sea level, Camel's Hump is Vermont's third highest mountain (tied with Mount Ellen) and rates as one of the finest hikes in the east. Try to climb this peak on a clear day. A mist-and-cloud enshrouded summit is a disappointing reward for the effort expended getting there.

Early French explorers gave the mountain its most appropriate name, the Couching Lion (Le Lion Couchant). From both east and west, its profile does resemble that of a resting lion. Victorians, who quivered at a subsequent name, "Camel's Rump," dubbed the mountain Camel's Hump.

There are a number of attractive paths to choose from in Camel's Hump trail system, approachable from either North Duxbury or Huntington Center. You can mix and match them to form a hike tailored to your own taste. The combination of trails described here forms a solid day's hiking over the steep, rugged terrain on the mountain's east side.

To reach the start of the Forestry Trail, your route most of the way up the mountain, follow VT 100 south out of Waterbury. Just past the US 2 junction, turn left by the sign for the Duxbury Elementary School. You will pass the red schoolhouse on the right. Continue straight on the gravel road for 5 miles. At that point, a buff-sided, black-roofed barn complex appears on the left. Turn south onto the gravel road just beyond the barns, and follow it 3.5 miles to its end at the Couching Lion Farm parking lot.

Camel's Hump State Park was established in 1969, in hopes of preserving at least one Green Mountain in a natural state. No camping is allowed and no fires are permitted on the trails. Green Mountain Club lodges are available for overnight use for a nominal charge.

At the far end of the parking lot, a pipe bubbles fresh water into a rock-walled well. The water is cold and delicious. If you have fluoridated water in your canteen, change it here.

The Forestry Trail starts beside this watering spot. Marked by pale blue blazes, the trail begins wide and flat. You will soon come to a register box and bulletin board; just beyond, a sign for the Forestry Trail points your way to the left.

The Forestry Trail is well maintained, as are all the trails on Camel's Hump. Long logs are positioned across the

path, beside trenched areas, to prevent
rain and melting snow runoff from
eroding the trail, which is unobstructed
by twigs, brush, or litter.

You now make a gradual ascent on
the broad packed-dirt trail, although tree
roots and boulders sometimes put in an
appearance. You will walk over many log
bridges; in summer and fall the streams
beneath them often dwindle to a trickle
or carry no water at all. At 1.5 miles, you
reach a set of trail signs. The Forestry
Trail goes right, and you are informed
that you have 1.8 miles to hike to reach
the Long Trail and 2.1 miles to cover to
reach Camel's Hump. The Dean Trail, on
your left, is where you will come down
later in the day.

The trail now becomes much more
demanding as it gets rockier and
steeper. At 2 miles you will come up to a
large and beautiful ledge. You will hike
along its left edge until you climb over it.
At 2.7 miles the Alpine Trail crosses
your path. Yellow blazes clearly mark
this route. Stay on the blue-blazed
Forestry Trail.

At 3.3 miles the Forestry and Long
trails meet in a large grassy clearing.
Turn left (south) and follow the Long
Trail to the summit. White or white-and-
orange blazes mark the way. The area
ahead is one of two arctic-alpine zones
in Vermont. The plants and grasses
(sedges) are rare and very fragile.
Footsteps kill them, so please walk only
on the rock-lined trail. Ranger-Naturalists
are on the mountain from May through
November to help hikers with any questions they may have about this area and
to render assistance if it is needed.

The Long Trail makes a winding, wind-

View of Camel's Hump from the East

buffeted ascent to the summit of Camel's Hump. Views extend north and south along the Green Mountains to Canada and Killington Peak, west to Lake Champlain and the Adirondacks, and east to the White Mountains.

The yellow-blazed Alpine Trail intersects the Long Trail just below the summit. Continue south on the Long Trail. This descent is steep, but you will be rewarded intermittently by views north to the cone of Camel's Hump and east to an eye-stretching vista of mountains and valleys. Underfoot, patches of boggy black mud offer the only relief from nearly continuous rocks and ledges.

As the Long Trail crosses the ridge and descends the east side of the mountain, beaver ponds become visible below. More climbing and sliding down over rock and scrub bring you to the junction of the Dean Trail after 4.5 miles of hiking.

Go left onto the blue-blazed Dean Trail. It is 1 mile from this point to its intersection with the Forestry Trail. The Dean Trail is mostly wet and muddy as it winds through the boggy area abutting the beaver ponds to the left. About .2 mile from the junction you'll come to Ridley Brook. The water courses quickly over and around its boulder-filled bed.

At the intersection of the Forestry and Dean trails, you are 1.5 miles from the parking area. Turn right onto the blue-blazed Forestry Trail and retrace your route. It is a very pleasant walk back to your car.

39

Mount Hunger

Class: IV
Distance (round trip): 3.8 miles
Hiking time: 4 hours
Vertical rise: 2,259 feet
USGS 7.5' Stowe

As the highest peak in the Worcester Range, 3,539-foot Mount Hunger commands superb views. Waterbury Valley and Reservoir nestle serenely to the west. Above and beyond, Green Mountain peaks extend south from Mount Mansfield. In all directions, mountains and valleys stretch before your eyes.

The Waterbury Center Trail is one of three routes to the summit; the other two begin in Shady Rill and Worcester. Turn off VT 100 at the sign for the Waterbury Center Post Office. Follow this road to its end. Go left at the stop sign, and then take the first right at the sign for Loomis Hill. Stay on this road for 3 miles and then turn right onto a dirt road. After approximately 200 feet, you will come to a tiny area on the left. Park here.

The path for Mount Hunger, marked by blue blazes, starts on an old grassy logging road bounded by red pine. These stately trees have an optimistic uplift to their branch tips. You can recognize them by their long (3 to 6-inches) needles in clusters of two. (Jack pine also has two-clustered needles, but they are 3/4 to 1 1/2 inches long.) the red pine's 2-to 3-inch cones grow directly on the twig.

Along the trail beyond the pines you'll find closed gentians. These tall plants have narrow leaves and usually grow in damp areas. Their bluish-purple flowers, which grow in clusters, appear in mid-to-late summer.

Climbing upward, the trail shifts from a logging road to a dirt and rock-strewn path through open woods. You hear a windlike sound to the left, which becomes louder as the trail swings upward to the right. Cresting a small knoll, you discover a rushing stream below.

At about the .2-mile point the trail appears to stop in front of a towering boulder. Go left and follow the path up around the rock. The trail swings sharply left around two tall red spruces and assumes a moderate pitch. It will maintain this angle all the way to the ledges near the summit. The footing is still soft and free of rocks and roots.

Leading upward through a typical hardwood forest of maple, beech, elm, and hemlock, the trail swings right and follows an old stream bed cluttered with logs and stones. The logs disappear, but the trail continues along the gully, sometimes in it and sometimes alongside it.

Walking through this area, you notice the yellow birches. Both sides of the trail are crowded with these buff-and silver-colored trees. Further along, as if to remind you that they are not to be forgotten, large, smooth-faced white birches dot the way.

At the 1-mile point the trail leads up over several long sections of ledge. Water trickles down the path, making it wet and slippery. Red blazes cross the trail, marking the state park boundary line.

The way has become increasingly rock filled and demands careful stepping. The trail swings right, under and around a knoll, and then rises steeply through a maze of white birches. The birch pattern has now been reversed: white dominate, and yellows have been left behind.

Balsam firs begin to appear as the path weaves over a network of roots and crosses a trickling stream at 1.2 miles. Trees are shorter, indicating that you are reaching higher elevations. The path bears left and flattens out for a short distance, providing a respite for wearied legs.

A second, slowly-moving stream crosses the path at the 1.5-mile mark.

View from the summit of Mount Elmore to Mount Hunger and the Worcester Range

Pause here for a cooling drink or a soothing footbath in the clear, cold water.

The dwarfed trees of the higher elevations offer less protection. Temperatures drop and winds blow increasingly stronger. Perpendicular ledge makes the climbing more difficult. Hands and walking sticks must aid your feet here. Hiking becomes a slow, step-at-a-time process.

The summit and surrounding area is barren, except for several dwarfed spruce no more than three feet high. Wind scours the area.

Return by the same route.

Elmore Mountain

Class: III
Distance (round trip): 3 miles
Hiking time: 2 1/4 hours
Vertical rise: 1,528 feet
USGS 15' Hyde Park

A day or two of varied outdoor recreation awaits you at Elmore State Park. Situated around the shores of Lake Elmore, the park includes a good-sized beach and a hiking trail to the summit of Elmore Mountain. Before or after hiking you'll have opportunities to camp or picnic; go swimming, boating, or fishing; and—if you didn't bring your own food—visit the refreshment stand.

Enter the park from VT 12, 4.3 miles southeast of Morrisville. To reach the hiking trail, proceed straight from the entrance booth—after paying the small day-use fee—toward the picnic area. The road swings left and begins to curve right, when a sharp right turn suddenly appears. Follow this road to a wood gate. Park on the right, just before the gate.

The trail to Elmore Mountain begins as a gravel road and winds gradually upward. Varied trees and flowers line the way. The trail becomes slightly steeper. Red blazes on trees to the left appear at the .5-mile mark. Don't mistake them for trail markers; they indicate the state park boundary.

A few steps farther along you will find a register box. Turn right here and walk up the split log steps. Pass between large beech trees with bark scarred by carved initials and names. The trail is wide and comfortable underfoot as it swings to parallel a small brook on the right. A short side path leads down to the water, which flows freely and tastes good.

As the way leads upward to the right, occasional log-braced trenches appear. Crossing the path, they divert runoff water before it can build up and damage the trail.

At .8 mile the smooth, flat trail splits. While the path straight ahead looks like the better traveled route, go right, following the steeper, rockier path. Just before you reach a group of large boulders, note that another trail comes in from the left. On your return, remember to stay left at this fork.

The trail winds right and then up to the left. It crosses two areas where logs have been placed atop wet spots. Beyond these logs another path intersects from the left. Just beyond this intersection, logs again provide firm footing across the wet trail. Remember after crossing this last set of logs on the way back that the left trail is the one to take.

The trail is still a pleasant dirt path,

relatively free of stones and roots. Steepening as it gains altitude, it goes through a wet, muddy area and approaches a high, steep ledge.

Climbing quite steeply, you will top a crest at the 1.2-mile mark and step into a surprisingly picturesque setting. Four beautiful white birches form a rectangular perimeter around a picnic table straight ahead. Behind and to the left of the grassy clearing a small cabin with stone chimney sits on a knoll overlooking Lake Elmore.

A fine view to the east across Lake Elmore opens from an overlook at the left edge of the clearing. If you are not anxious to climb the very steep and narrow .2-mile trail to the summit, this view provides an acceptable substitute.

The trail follows white painted arrows up the ledge to the summit. Although the climb is very demanding, the reward at the top will make the effort worthwhile.

Climb the lookout tower for a beautiful view. With the exception of the Worcester Range immediately to the south, Elmore Mountain is the highest point in the area. You gaze out over endless miles of rolling hills and manicured farms separated by patches of dark green trees.

The black and white forms of cows dot the open fields and the sun reflects off silos and metal roofs. The impression is one of awesome vastness; the mood, peaceful and relaxed as you look to the horizons.

Blake Pond

Class: II
Distance (round trip): 5.8 miles
Hiking time: 2 1/2 hours
Vertical rise: 580 feet
USGS 15' Lyndonville

Black Pond is one of many primitive ponds cradled within Willoughby State Forest's 6,700 acres. The trail to it, like others in the forest, provides a nice opportunity to quietly enjoy nature and, at the same time, limber up your muscles for more strenuous hikes. It also offers an excellent introduction to Willoughby's attractive trail system, where you can easily spend hours.

To reach the Blake Pond Trail, drive to the Willoughby State Forest parking area off US 5. It is located 5.5 miles south of the junction of US 5 and VT 16 in Barton and 7.2 miles north of the junction of US 5 and VT 5A in West Burke. Walk south from the parking lot and turn left onto the dirt road.

Follow this road to the sturdy, slatted, wooden bridge crossing the outlet of Bean Pond. If you look southeast across the pond, you'll have a good view of Norris Mountain. Shortly beyond the bridge the dirt road forks. Bear left on the rocky narrow road that makes its way up a small grade. At the top it too forks, and a brown signboard etched with white letters guides you to the right toward Blake Pond.

Beeches, sugar maples, and white birches parade beside the trail. The way

is intermittently dark and light as trees touch branches overhead, blocking much of the sky light. Then they are interrupted by groups of waist-high goldenrod and wood asters. Butterflies and bees dart and swoop among the blossoms.

Much of the way the grade here is steep. The trail turns sharply to the right and continues looping uphill. Watch for the tiny toads that scuttle about your feet (they seem to get underfoot before you notice them).

At .9 mile tall grass and spreading shrubs start to overrun the path as it levels off, giving your muscles a well-earned rest. In another .2 mile, however, you'll climb the steepest grade of this rutted, rocky road. Ferns grow luxuriantly along the trail. Although there are no trail markers, the roadway is so obvious that you won't get lost.

A number of young and mature striped maples fill this area. These slender trees can be readily identified by their large, three-lobed leaves and smooth black-and-white streaked bark.

After 1.7 miles the trail winds to the left and widens, and the woods itself becomes more open. Walking is less arduous than it has been. More brown and white signboards direct you at 2.8 miles. On the right, one points straight ahead to Blake Pond. To the left another aims you to Wheeler Mountain.

The road to Blake Pond, which you follow, forks a short distance beyond the signs, and a sign between the two arms of the fork indicates that you have ar-

rived at the pond. The water is visible through the trees to the right. If you approach quietly, you may surprise a wading blue heron or feeding ducks. If you like to fish, Blake Pond is also a great place to try your newest fishing pole.

Return to your car by the same route.

Mount Pisgah

Class: III
Distance (round trip): 6.9 miles
Hiking time: 4 1/2 hours
Vertical rise: 1,491 feet
USGS 15' Lyndonville

Sheer-faced Mount Pisgah forms the towering southeastern perimeter of Lake Willoughby. Its trails are noted for their prime views of the lake, the northern Green Mountains, and the Burke Mountain-Victory Bog Wilderness. This loop hike takes you up the south side of Pisgah, over the summit, back down the north side, and finally along the base by Lake Willoughby.

The South Trail begins on VT 5A, 5.6 miles south of the junction of VT 5A and VT 16 in Westmore. You'll see the brown and white "South Trail" sign at the eastern side of the highway approximately .5 mile south of Lake Willoughby. Leave your car in the area directly across the road.

The trail leads you down to a couple of well-built log bridges constructed by the Vermont Youth Conservation Corps. This program employs youths aged fifteen to eighteen on Conservation projects that help develop, maintain, and improve forest, wildlife, and recreational resources on public lands. In addition to work experience, corps members learn the hows and whys of natural resource management.

Beyond the bridges, the trail is well marked with blue blazes. The wide,

relatively smooth path winds its way through brilliant white birches and begins a climb through open woods. Boulders form islands in the trail. Walking is sometimes easy and sometimes rugged, especially over moss-covered rocks. If you'll believe a favorite uncle's tale about Indian blood causing the rocks to turn green, this area must have been a major battlefield!

In .2 mile the trail swings ninety degrees to the left at a brown and white sign. The steep grade persists as you pick your way over rocks in the path. The path eventually widens and smooths out, but continues its upward climb.

In .5 mile the trail switches back right, then left, and proceeds up a rocky embankment. Near the top, a 40-foot-long spur on the left leads to the first of the open views from the South Trail. A second area 300 feet farther along offers open western views.

Leaving the second vista, walk upward to the right. Lovely white birch flank the trail, sparkling among the surrounding greens and greys of the forest. At .8 mile a hand-painted white and black sign guides you to Pulpit Rock, at an elevation of 1,710 feet. Views west are of Mount Hor and Wheeler Mountain; the southern end of Lake Willoughby lies directly below.

The largest fish ever caught in Vermont came from Lake Willoughby's deep waters. On May 8, 1960, Leon E. Hopkins landed a forty-six-inch lake trout that weighed thirty-four pounds and had a twenty-five-inch girth. The fish was so heavy that Leon had to beach it to get it out of the water. This record specimen can be seen at the Leon E. Hopkins & Son Insurance Agency on Church Street in Lyndonville, Vermont.

The rest of the climb to the summit is unrelentingly steep. It passes over and around boulders and makes a sharp swing left around a massive elm. The white birches give way to beeches and maples, and the path picks its way through stone-strewn areas. At 1.2 miles a medium-sized, blue-blazed boulder bisects the path.

Balsam fir begin to populate the slopes as the grey, broad-leaf forest melds into the green alpine one. Ledge appears and trees become abbreviated in height. Grey mica-flecked sand crunches underfoot as the climb over bare ledge steepens. Natural depressions in the rock and clinging roots provide good footholds. At 1.6 miles you'll be en-

couraged by a group of signs indicating that the true summit is only 500 feet away. The heavily wooded peak offers no views.

Leave the summit via the North Trail (also blue blazed). About .2 mile from the top you will reach the spur trail to Lookout #1 (West Lookout). Wind your way to the left for awesome views of Lake Willoughby and surrounding peaks. Mount Hor is the closest to the west. Wheeler Mountain is the rock-faced peak to the northwest. The total view extends sixty miles, from Lake Memphremagog and Jay Peak to Camel's Hump and beyond.

Rejoin the North Trail and continue a short distance to the spur for Lookout #2 (North Lookout). Turn left. White signs with black arrows guide you along this narrow, curving trail.

Retrace your steps to the North Trail and turn left. This cool, shaded path descends gradually. Low bushes threaten to choke portions of it at times. The way becomes steeper and leads over black spongy earth past several massive moss-covered stumps. The path sharply bends to the right and then drops steeply left. At a fork, the Long Pond Trail goes right. Stay on the North

View across Lake Willoughby to Mount Pisgah

Trail to the left. The path descends steeply and rapidly. This is prime ankle-spraining territory, so pick your way carefully.

Finally, at a less extreme angle, the trail courses along a small gully over an old stream bed. At 3.5 miles you must rock-hop across a clear running stream. The trail parallels this stream and turns right as the gurgling quiets in the background. A second stream crosses the path shortly thereafter.

The North Trail continues over gentle hills and gullies. It turns sharply left and begins the steeper descent to VT 5A. Once at the road you have a pleasant 2.7-mile walk along Lake Willoughby to your start.

Devil's Gulch

Class: II
Distance (round trip): 5 miles
Hiking time: 3 hours
Vertical rise: 780 feet
USGS 15' Jay Peak; USGS 15' Hyde Park

This rough gouge in the earth abounds with ferns and moss-covered rocks. It is regarded by the Green Mountain Club as one of the most beautiful, secluded spots of the Long Trail. Its forbidding name adds a primitive lure all its own.

The access road to the portion of the Long Trail leading to Devil's Gulch is VT 118, the Eden-Belvidere Highway. Drive west from Eden 4.8 miles or east from Belvidere Center 6.1 miles. Watch for the green and white Long Trail sign and arrow on the south side of the highway. There is limited parking in a grassy off-road area on the north side of the road. (Hike 44, to Belvidere Mountain, also begins at this point.)

Cross to the road's south side and follow the white blazes of the Long Trail up the embankment and into the woods. The path winds gently through young, lean trees. The trail then enters open woods. Its upward course is still gentle, and few roots or stones roughen the way.

A variety of greenery begins to edge the path. One of the most striking specimens is striped maple, with its smooth, greenish bark vividly striped by black and white. In May its clusters of yellow flowers appear. The leaves are

Deep within Devil's Gulch

large, generally with three main lobes.

The trail twists easily up, over, and down gentle knolls. At a small clearing marked by patches of wet black mud and large fallen trees, watch carefully for the white blazes as the path winds left. Shrubbery chokes the trail and thorned blackberry bushes tug at your legs. You must thrust your way through this thick growth and over wet areas.

A steep downslope may require some careful side-stepping. Generally, you lose elevation on your trek to Devil's Gulch. It's the exact opposite of climbing a mountain: the return trip (via the same route) will be the more trying one.

Soon the path crosses a fast-running stream. This is one of three dependable water sources on the trail. At the 2-mile point the route that you have been hiking

on joins an old unused section of the Long Trail. Always stay on the well-marked white-blazed Long Trail.

You cross another fast-flowing brook shortly. After winding steeply upward the trail approaches Ritterbush Camp. This small frame building was constructed in 1933 and can accommodate eight. (A toilet is provided—up a short trail to the left.) Walk to the back right corner of the cabin and continue hiking.

The way leads steadily upward to a ninety-degree turn where a white sign points left. Here, you may step out onto a small overlook to the right. Below, a stream courses through the middle of a tree-and-shrub-choked gully.

Wind down to the right over a log foot-bridge into this gully. A miniature water-fall appears to the left. Hold your cupped hands beneath its flow and enjoy a refreshing drink.

Just ahead is a brief but rugged climb over moss-covered boulders and gnarled roots. The path levels again as stepping stones offer footing across a dank-smelling wet area. Ahead, massive hunks of rock form an A-shaped tunnel. After passing between them, you reach Devil's Gulch.

A jumble of boulders makes hiking a challenge. Above, ledge rises straight and steep on both sides. Ferns feather the surfaces of many of these gargantuan boulders. Cave-like depressions lurk among the rocks forming the gulch walls. Stand still and survey these surroundings. The feeling is a primeval one—time seems to have stood still.

The Devil's Gulch is breathtaking—and has a special appeal if you've been climbing a lot of mountains recently. It is such a change. And it even remains attractive in a heavy fog.

Return via the same route.

Belvidere Mountain

Class: III
Distance (round trip): 5.6 miles
Hiking time: 4 hours
Vertical rise: 2,080 feet
USGS 15' Jay Peak

Belvidere Mountain is better known for its asbestos mines than for the expansive views available from its summit. Since 1936, when the Ruberoid Company began systematically mining its slopes, Belvidere has been a leader in producing asbestos. In the mid-1950s this one mountain yielded ninety-six percent of all the asbestos mined in the United States. An active mine at the eastern base of the mountain still supplies asbestos for shingles, cement, theater curtains, firemen's suits, brake linings, pipe coverings, and other products.

This hike begins opposite the one to Devil's Gulch (see Hike 43). The Long Trail crosses VT 118 at the high point of land located 4.8 miles west of Eden and 6.1 miles east of Belvidere Center on the Eden-Belvidere Highway. Look along the south side of the highway for the white and green Long Trail sign. There is limited parking on the north side of the road.

The Long Trail leads into the woods, parallels Frying Pan Brook, and then continues over old VT 118, crossing the fast-flowing brook in the process. As you head into the woods you pass over several wet, boggy areas. Long logs aid

the footing through this thickly muddied section. The path swings upward to the right around a yellow birch and continues to a large maple, which splits the trail. A former logging road leads right and the Long Trail goes left. Keep on the Long Trail.

The way steepens moderately, as the gully through which Frying Pan Brook runs appears below to the left. The trail keeps company with the brook for quite a distance, alternately paralleling and swinging away from it.

After .2 mile an old logging road crosses the trail diagonally and dips down to the brook. The brook's waters slither and slide over long stretches of flat rock.

The path intersects another logging road and continues along it to the left. The track suddenly becomes wider and flat. A small trickle of water muddies the trail just before it takes a sharp swing to the right. It leads into a small, low, wet area and seems to stop. Although the trail is not well marked, it goes right here and climbs over root-formed steps.

As the grade flattens out, the trail becomes bumpy with rocks while it parallels the brook on the left. It crisscrosses and rises steeply alongside this miniature wilderness river. The water cascades through slender gouges, over rocks, and into shallow pools before gushing downward again.

More wet patches appear. The path crests a moderate slope and passes over two grassy roads in quick succession. Trail sides overflow with fern, hobblebush, and wood sorrel.

The way becomes very steep as it leads over roots and rocks. Trees thin out drastically at the top of the incline. A startlingly large patch of sky suddenly appears above. You are now approximately halfway to the top of Belvidere Mountain.

Leveling out a bit, the trail crosses an overgrown logging road. Trees become shorter as the way winds upward. It dips down into a small, very wet gully and finds firmer footing on old logs. You cross still another old road as the trail passes through an open area and weaves left.

Narrowing to a mere footpath, the trail swings steeply right and passes over a long slab of ledge. It tunnels through thick stands of evergreens and is bathed in their fragrance and then picks its way slowly over and around slippery, moss-covered rocks and roots.

Just before a four-way intersection at Belvidere Saddle between the two peaks of Belvidere Mountain watch closely for a yellow blaze on the left side of the trail. The unmarked Forester's Trail, your route to the top, is just beyond it on the right marked with a blue arrow painted on a rock. It brings you in .2 mile to the main summit. The way is very straight

View of Belvidere Mountain showing the asbestos mine

and moderately steep.

An old deserted lookout platform and a watchman's hut greet you at the summit. Climb the tower and enjoy the unfolding views.

To the east are the peaks around Lake Willoughby: Bald Mountain, Mount Pisgah, and Mount Hor, with the White Mountains of New Hampshire extending to the horizon. Swinging south, the Green Mountains are visible, Mount Mansfield and Camel's Hump, particularly so. The Cold Hollow Mountains sit to the west, while Jay Peak and Big Jay rise prominently in the north. To the right of these twin peaks are Owl's Head and other Canadian peaks in the vicinity of Lake Memphremagog.

Return to your car by the same route.

Jay Peak

Class: IV
Distance (round trip): 3.4 miles
Hiking time: 3 hours
Vertical rise: 1,661 feet
USGS 15' Jay Peak

If you are striving to become a south-to-north end-to-ender on the Long Trail, Jay Peak's summit leaves you only ten miles short of your goal. A primitive wilderness until snow falls, Jay then transforms itself into a bustling center of winter activity as one of the most popular ski areas in northern Vermont. Avid skiers think nothing of traveling hundreds of miles to ride its aerial tramway and make as many runs as time and money allow.

The Long Trail (your route to Jay's summit) crosses the Jay-Montgomery Center Road (VT 242) at the top of a long, steep grade between the two towns. The hike to Jay Peak begins on the north side of the highway, 5.1 miles west of Jay village and 6.7 miles east of Montgomery Center. The Jay Peak Ski area road is 1.3 miles east of this spot.

The Long Trail, to Jay Peak, marked by white blazes, begins across the road from the parking area. The Atlas Valley Shelter sits on a knoll just above road level. The Atlas Plywood Division, over whose land the trail passes here, provided this small plywood lean-to. Green Mountain Club members erected it in 1967. It is designed for day use by picnickers and hikers—but it can accommodate three or four people overnight.

The trail begins as a narrow path leading upward through stands of young white birches. After a few minutes' walk, you approach a brown and white sign. The Long Trail continues straight ahead while a side trail leads left to Jay Camp, .2 mile distant.

The way leads upward over an old stream bed. Rock faces are crinkled with moss and tiny pools of water dampen the trail. Beautiful yellow birches suddenly catch your eye as they parade down the hillside and across the path. They glimmer silvery yellow from deep within the woods.

As another side trail from Jay Camp enters on the left, yellow birches begin to mix with the white birches to which they eventually give way. Hobblebush lines the path. Deer like to feed on the twigs and buds of this three-to eight-foot-high shrub. Large white clusters of flowers appear in May and June, while pearl-shaped fruit develop in August and change from red to black at maturity. The leaves also change to a deep magenta color in the fall.

The path leads upward to the left, then dips quickly. Ferns, moss, hobblebush, and striped maple combine to produce heavy green sidegrowth. Slightly higher, common wood sorrel appears near ground level. It has three compound leaves and at a quick glance might be mistaken for clover. Its leaves taste tangy and refreshing.

Edging along the hillside, the slope of the path becomes more gradual. It continues like this for a fair distance, allowing legs and lungs to relax a bit. Then, winding up through spruce and balsam, the way becomes rockier and steeper. Bunches of shining club moss cluster around tree bottoms. They look like small gardens of cactus nestled between the trees.

A new trail, still marked with white blazes, parallels a large ski slope. This trail was much needed, as it keeps you in the woods. Damp spots make the going slippery at times. The Christmas-tree smell of balsam fills the air and accompanies you upward.

Just below the summit the way leads out onto a large ski trail cut through the timberland. The 100-foot-wide swath looks like the aftermath of a glacier that flattened everything in its path. Watch closely for white arrows and blazes where the trail crosses the slope and re-enters the woods.

The trail snakes through low scrub growth of spruce and balsam. You pass the small, metal-roofed hut of the ski patrol on the right and begin the final climb to the summit over bumpy ledge and two-foot-high alpine forests.

Cresting the final ledge, you'll find the view is breath-taking, looking out to all directions and taking in rolling hills, towering peaks, flat farmland, winding roads, and long lakes.

Eastward, the view includes Lake Memphremagog; to the west, the Champlain Valley. The Green Mountains can bee seen stretching southward as far as Lincoln Peak, while Owl's Head and other Canadian mountains rise to the north.

Your return is via the same trail.

Stratton Mountain and Pond

Time allowed: 2 days, 1 night
Class: II & III
Distance (round trip): 13.2 miles
Hiking time: 7 hours
Vertical rise: 1,981 feet
USGS 15' Londonderry

Your itinerary for this backpacking trip includes the 3,936-foot south peak of Stratton Mountain, trailside views of beaver ponds, and a night on the shores of Stratton Pond, the largest and one of the most attractive bodies of water on the Long Trail. All in all, it's a great hike.

(Stratton Mountain's north peak, which houses the upper station of the Stratton Mountain Chair Lift, is bypassed on the hike. Should you want to visit this area, follow the .8-mile spur trail leading north from the fire tower on the south peak.)

First Day

Arlington-West Wardsboro Road to Stratton View Shelter

Class: III
Distance: 6.2 miles
Hiking time: 3 1/2 hours
Vertical rise: 1,616 feet

The Stratton Mountain Trail starts on the Arlington-West Wardsboro Road. Driving east from Arlington to the trail is not recommended, due to rough road conditions. Drive west from VT 100 in West Wardsboro. Signs to Stratton and Arlington mark the turn. After 5.2 miles you'll see the blue sign for the Stratton

Mountain Trail on the right. Just before the trail a small opening on the right leads to adequate off-the-road parking.

This rather rocky trail soon leads past Webster Shelter at .1 mile. The structure was named for Daniel Webster, who delivered a campaign speech nearby in 1840. At that time, Stratton Mountain rose above one of the most prosperous lumbering and agricultural districts of the state. The Stratton Turnpike added to the area's distinctiveness; it was the road taken by Boston's "best citizens" enroute to summer vacations at Saratoga Springs.

This prestigious area was selected as the site for a large Whig campaign rally for Harrison and Tyler. A fifty-by-one-hundred-foot log cabin was constructed just off the highway to house the gathering. With Daniel Webster as the orator, the gathering drew a crowd of 15,000 persons (the exact count has been questioned, however, because of the tremendous amounts of hard cider that flowed throughout the proceedings).

Beyond the shelter, the trail forks. Go left on the blue-blazed Stratton Mountain Trail. Trickling water wets the path as it winds upward at a moderate grade through many evergreens. Telephone lines accompany you from time to time. Bear left at the fork after .5 mile. Beyond this point the path follows a long, direct rise up the side of a hill. The way slides between giant rocks as it leads upward.

Continuing through hardwoods, this well-marked and cleared trail passes just beneath the ridge line on the west side of the slope; then it cuts across the ridge to the east side and bends left. At 1.7 miles, it follows an arrow and makes a sharp swing up to the right.

After a short, steep section, the way resumes its moderate pitch. Grasses and wood asters flourish in open areas. The path crosses a brook at 2 miles and turns right just beyond it. Telephone lines go left here.

Rougher and steeper, the trail carves its way up through more evergreens. At 2.2 miles a grassy trail forks to the left. Continue straight on the Stratton Mountain Trail.

You emerge onto an old trail at 2.3 miles. Directly ahead a comfortable log bench (the work of some thoughtful person) is situated at just the right spot and welcomes your use. The water from a pipe is drinkable.

You reach the summit of Stratton Mountain after a climb of 2.5 miles. Two small buildings and a fire tower occupy this area. The rangers are in residence from the end of April to the end of October. (Please note that camping is not permitted on the summit or elsewhere along this trail, except at the designated shelters.)

Fantastic views await you from the top of the tower. The panorama is unusual, because you are able to see some of the more famous peaks from angles that isolate them against the horizons. Equinox Mountain, highest of the Taconic Range, is on the west. Northeast is Mount Ascutney. New Hampshire's Mount Monadnock dominates the southeastern skyline. South is Somerset Reservoir and Mount Snow. Glastenbury Mountain rises in the southwestern corner.

Beyond and to the left of the tower, the blue-blazed Stratton Mountain Trail descends from the summit. Water seeps onto the path, making the way black and mirey. The grade shortly becomes more gradual as the trail winds down through open woods. After crossing a fast-flowing brook—the water is drinkable—at 3.8 miles, the descent becomes even more gentle.

Beside the trail at 4.1 miles are the remains of an old log camp. Giant moss-green logs lie in a tumble to the right of the path. Another .5 mile of hiking takes you across a slow-running brook to a beaver pond. Crossing another stream, you can watch its waters flow into yet another pond on the right. As the trail angles left, take time to look for the beaver lodge at the back of this pond.

After winding along above this pond, the way dips down to meet an old road. Swing left and follow the road as it passes through the tall grass of open fields and over several streams. With the passage of time this open setting will become a forest landscape. At the 5-mile point, branch left at the fork and leave the road. Almost immediately you make an angled swing to the right.

Shortly before winding down to Stratton Pond, the path travels near another beaver pond. At 5.5 miles you reach the trail junction at the pond's shore. Go right on the North Shore Trail. This path edges close to the waters of Stratton Pond for most of its length. Soon you pass a short spur on the right leading to a primitive camping area.

The North Shore Trail swings sharply left across a long tree, which forms a sturdy footbridge. A seemingly endless tangle of roots must then be maneuvered over and around. More sun-

TRAIL
442

*Stratton
Pond*

Willis Ross
BM Camp
2559

NATIONNA

LONG

N

3875 ×

2647

2603

(APPALACHIAN TRAIL)

TRAIL

Stratton
Lookout Tower   3936

Stratton Mountain

2431

East Br

LONG

STRATTON

TRAIL

LONG

2400

2900

2470

0   1
mile

TRAIL
2229

Daniel Webster
Historical Mon

LONG

TRAIL

BM
2312

P

JEEP

Deerfield TRAIL

2284

Grout

Stratton Mtn

bleached logs carry you across boggy areas. Soon good views of Stratton Mountain open back across the pond. The lower north peak is to the left, the higher south peak with its fire tower is to the right.

At 6.2 miles you reach Stratton View Shelter. The mountain fills the skyline across the pond. A Green Mountain Club caretaker collects a nominal fee for overnight use of this three-sided, dirt-floored shelter.

Vondell and Bigelow shelters are .3 and .5 mile further on. Although their settings do not have Stratton View's appeal, they do offer the added luxury of a floor.

Second Day

Stratton View Shelter to Arlington-West Wardsboro Road

Class: II
Distance: 7 miles
Hiking time: 3 1/2 hours
Vertical rise: 365 feet

To make your stay at Stratton View Shelter worthwhile, get up early today. Allow plenty of time for enjoying this scenic spot. You might see early morning animal activity close to the pond's edges. If the weather cooperates, you'll greet the sun as it rises over the mountain and paints the pond red.

When you are ready to depart, take the North Shore Trail to the right. It passes over several boggy areas as it follows the pond's shore line. After .1 mile you reach an intersection filled with many signs. Follow the white blazes of the Long Trail south to the pond's shore. It goes left and cuts across the Stratton Pond outlet via long logs wired together.

On land again, the path winds through very damp areas. Long series of walkalongs provide firmer footing. Tangled roots lace the trail whenever you step on hard ground.

At .3 mile you come to the Vondell Shelter. The International Paper Company constructed this lean-to in 1967. It has bunk space for six to eight hikers. The trail continues along the water's edge to the Bigelow Shelter at .5 mile. This lean-to sleeps six in bunks and might be an alternate stopping place if you are hiking during a busy weekend.

Continuing its water-edged route, the trail enters a clearing at .7 mile. Just

View to Stratton Mountain from Bromley Mountain

beyond is Willis Ross Camp. This structure can sleep twelve and has a spring 30 feet to the north. From the clearing follow the sign for the Long Trail South to the right. Leaving the pond behind, you climb gradually up over a mixture of rocks and roots.

A sign announcing the distance to the Arlington-West Wardsboro Road stops the trail at .8 mile. The way swings sharply right here and begins a bumpy journey. It dips in spots, but remains fairly level. You cross a small brook at 1.4 miles and turn left.

After a gradual climb the trail levels off again. The thin woods are filled with ferns and shining club moss. Needles cover the trail as you begin to wander through spruces and balsam firs.

There is little change in elevation as the trail log-hops over boggy areas and twists between evergreens. Frequent short dips and rises hinder you from maintaining a steady stride. Don't just pass by the damp boggy areas. These are prime spots for finding animal tracks. Deer, bear, raccoon, bobcat, porcupine—any of these animals might have passed this way recently. Many older, dead trees have visible holes in their trunks. Made either by woodpeckers or branches breaking off, they provide homes for tree swallows, chickadees, nuthatches, wrens, bluebirds, squirrels, raccoons, and martens.

Topping a short slope, the path becomes alternately smooth and rocky. It dips down a short steep bank and spans a large, boggy area atop logs. At 2.3 miles the trail crosses an old grassy road and bears left. After a gradual climb it becomes flatter, smoother, and muddier.

Beginning a long series of bends and straightaways, the trail passes through unchanging woods. This area provides opportunities to do several things while walking along. Try brushing up on tree identification. Many of the hardwoods common to New England fill these woods.

At the 4-mile point the trail diagonally crosses an old road. It proceeds gradually downward over squishy terrain. Leveling out, the way swings sharply right and drops down to the Arlington-West Wardsboro Highway.

Turn left onto the dirt road (it changes to tar farther on). From here you have a 2.7-mile walk back to your car. Unlike the quick dips and rises of the trail, the smoothness of the road will let you stretch your leg muscles. You'll be able to set a good pace from here on.

Middlebury Gap to Brandon Gap

Time allowed: 2 days, 1 night
Class: III & IV
Distance (one way): 9.8 miles
Hiking time: 7 1/2 hours
Vertical rise: 2,535 feet
USGS 7.5' Mount Carmel; USGS 7.5' Bread Loaf

You'll hike up and down five different peaks with continuing panoramas highlighting the way during this two-day trip. There will be plenty of time for stops at the many lookoffs along the trail.

In 1915 Colonel Joseph Battell, an early spokesman for conservation of Vermont's forests, bequeathed to Middlebury College most of the land over which this hike passes. During the late 1800s when his friends were paying thousands of dollars for paintings, Battell was buying thousands of acres of land for $.10 to $.50 cents an acre. As the rates rose, he bought hundreds more at $1.25 per acre.

Responsibility for maintaining this section of the Long Trail (your route for the hike) rests with the U.S. Forest Service. The Middlebury College Mountain Club, however, does the actual work. The trail is extremely well marked, easy to follow, and well cleared of debris.

First Day

Middlebury Gap to Sucker Brook Shelter

Class: III
Distance: 4.4 miles
Hiking time: 3 1/2 hours
Vertical rise: 1,420 feet

To reach Middlebury Gap, drive 6.4 miles west from Hancock or 5.6 miles east from Ripton on the Robert Frost Memorial Drive (VT 125). The brown and yellow "Long Trail—Green Mountain National Forest" sign on the north side of the road is the landmark to watch for. Across the highway is a large parking area. (You'll finish this hike about 8 miles due south at VT 73; remember to arrange for transportation back to your car.)

From the south side of VT 125, climb the white-blazed Long Trail into the woods. The grade quickly eases as the thin tree cover stretches outward. A ski slope appears through scattered trees to the left, and the path parallels another slope on the right. Continuing moderately upward, the trail crosses intersecting ski slopes and enters the woods beyond. White markers clearly show the way.

The grade becomes more gradual and the walking easier. Suddenly the trail drops and makes a long descent to Lake Pleiad Shelter. You have come .3 mile from Middlebury Gap.

A white arrow guides you past the shelter's left side. Cross an open ski slope and enter the woods again. The trail flattens out as it passes through thick stands of birches and striped maples and a gathering of spruces.

Long logs carry you across a brook as you approach a trail intersection. The blue-blazed spur to Lake Pleiad exits straight ahead. Turn sharply left on the Long Trail. As the pitch increases the path becomes rougher. Leveling out, the trail intersects an old logging road. Watch carefully for the white markers. Cross diagonally to the right and back into the woods. Then follow the arrow to the left.

Rising steeply, the path crosses two more ski trails. From the sloping ledge on the second trail it runs sharply right and zigzags up a steep, roughly cleared slope. At its crest, follow the beaten path up to the left. It quickly joins with the blue-blazed spur leading right to Worth Mountain Lodge. Bear left with the Long Trail.

The way continues upward to the Robert Frost Lookout. The sloping hillside opens up before you and offers spectacular views to the northeast. Mountains near and far seem to roll upon each other like gentle waves.

After a short, moderate climb the path flattens out. It winds cozily through stands of trail-hugging evergreens. With the flatness comes wetness. Boggy areas must be gingerly negotiated.

After dropping over smooth ledge, the dirt path begins a long, moderate ascent over occasional ledge and roots. The aroma of spruce and balsam enlivens your senses. Partial views of nearby mountains are available through thin trees to the left.

A slight descent is followed by more level, boggy areas. Beginning another climb, the path rises steeply over ledge and clinging roots. At 2.5 miles it enters the small clearing at Eastern Lookoff. Neighboring peaks sit atop one another as they stretch into the distance. Another .1 mile brings you to the top of Worth Mountain, elevation 3,234 feet. The heavily wooded summit offers no view.

During the long, steep descent from Worth Mountain, you have continuous panoramic views of the Green Mountains stretching southward. Killington Peak is particularly prominent. This entire section of the Long Trail is a haven for partridge. If you are lucky, you might surprise this wise game bird atop a stump or rock while it performs its strutting, spring courtship ritual. More probably, some of them will see you first and rocket upward through thick tree

Sucker Brook Shelter

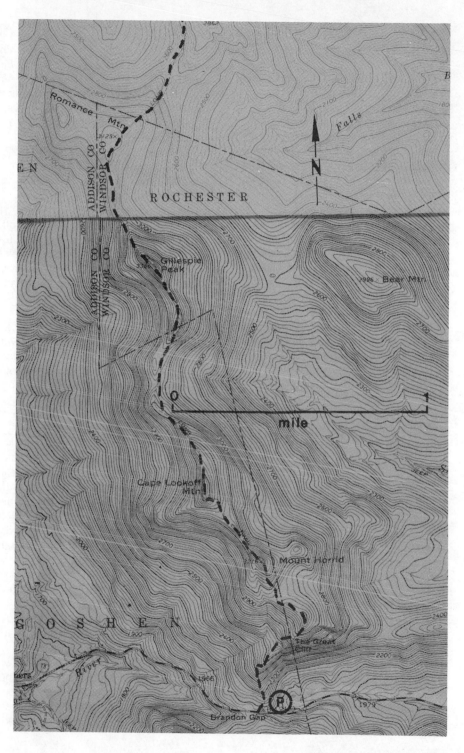

branches. You will often hear the powerful beating of their wings, but never see them at all.

The path levels out after its descent from Worth Mountain. It follows a series of dips and rises and begins a long, gradual descent through thinned-out woods. Dropping over a short ledge, the way swings left through a stand of beeches. These stately trees seem to improve with age. The smooth, light grey bark gives them an elegance their rougher-barked companions lack. Then hardwood forests flank the path as it rises moderately. Glacial boulders become prominent, and shoulder-high spruces edge the trail as the hillside slopes steeply away.

At 4.3 miles the trail crosses a brook flowing quickly down the sloping hill. The Sucker Brook Shelter is just beyond at 4.4 miles. Its green floor can easily sleep six to eight hikers. Water is available just to the south where Sucker Brook passes under the Long Trail.

Second Day

Sucker Brook Shelter to Brandon Gap.

Class: IV
Distance: 5.4 miles
Hiking time: 4 hours
Vertical rise: 1,115 feet

Before you leave Sucker Brook Shelter, remember to fill your water containers at the brook. Ahead of you today is some steady trekking to four summits and, finally, a rugged descent from the Great Cliff of Mount Horrid.

A short way south of Sucker Brook Shelter, the Long Trail intersects the Sucker Brook Trail. This blue-blazed trail leads west down the valley to the Ripton-Goshen Road. Stay on the Long Trail.

Making its way to Romance Mountain, the path leads through Romance Gap. Twisting and turning, it climbs steeply over rocks and roots. After cresting this long slope, the path levels out. Shining club moss gleams against the brownish-red carpet of evergreen spills.

A delicious aroma engulfs you as the trail passes through darkened groves of conifers. After more climbing between moss-covered rocks and logs, you emerge onto the eastern summit of Romance Mountain (1.4 miles from Sucker Brook Shelter). There is no view from the tree-covered top of this 3,125-foot peak.

Swing left; the trail drops down off the summit. Very shortly, you come to a fork where a 50-foot spur leads to a western overlook. As you continue south on the Long Trail a view to the east also appears.

Walkalongs aid you through this jumbled area of twisting trail, logs, and roots. This section of the trail follows the ridge line. However, views to the east and west are screened by stands of trees. Occasional spurs lead left and right off the path to overlooks.

After 2.2 miles the narrow trail leads across ledges and upward to the 3,307-foot summit of White Rocks Mountain. From this vantage point you can look to the north and see Romance Mountain. As you begin the descent, green waves of mountains roll south and westward.

The way down is again steep and over rough sections for a bit. The grade then becomes fairly level and proceeds through fir forests. The path moves gradually upward over patches of ledge to another small clearing, the 3,298-foot summit of Cape Lookoff Mountain. A short spur leads west from this heavily treed summit to an overview.

Leaving Cape Lookoff, you wind your way down over more ledges. Continue more gradually downward through stands of birches surrounded by leafy ferns. Then, going up over roots and rocks, you begin a sustained ascent to 3,150-foot Mount Horrid. From here you can look back to Cape Lookoff Mountain and enjoy your recent accomplishment.

The descent from the summit of Mount Horrid to the Great Cliff is a rough one over steep areas of jumbled rock. Walkalongs provide welcome support across particularly boggy areas. There is flatter walking through an area of gnarled birches just before your arrival at the Mount Horrid Lookoff sign (4.8 miles from the start of the day's hiking). Caution rules here. The cliff face drops sharply off and falls 600 feet to the gap below. The highway looks like a slender ribbon as it winds through Bran-don Gap. Above it, the Green Mountain chain stretches southward.

Returning from the cliff, go left and follow the white blazes down to Brandon Gap. This .6-mile descent is extremely precipitous in places, dropping very steeply over ledge and roots before leveling out. The sides along the entire descent are forested with sparkling paper birches.

The trail becomes more gradual. After a final easy descent, you emerge from the woods and walk through shrubbery and grass to VT 73. To the east, Rochester and VT 100 are 9.7 miles away; to the west, Brandon and US 7 are 8.2 miles distant.

The Coolidge Range

Time allowed: 3 days, 2 nights
Class: III & IV
Distance (one way): 16.7 miles
Hiking time: 12 hours
Vertical rise: 4,693 feet
USGS 7.5' Killington, USGS 7.5' Pico Peak; USGS 7.5' Rutland

This backpacking trip principally on the Long Trail takes you through the northern mountains of the Coolidge Range. Two of Vermont's most popular peaks are the main attractions here. Pico Peak (elevation 3,957 feet) raises its cone-shaped dome high above Sherburne Pass. South of Pico, Killington Peak (elevation 4,241 feet), the second highest mountain in Vermont, has a more pointed profile.

Most of the steep climbing will be done during the first day and a half. During the second half of this trip, continuous downhill walking puts more strain on the knees than the thighs. You'll have plenty of time for scenery gazing without having to be concerned about hiking time.

First Day

Sherburne Pass to Cooper Lodge

Class: IV
Distance: 5.8 miles
Hiking time: 4 1/2 hours
Vertical rise: 3,287 feet

The Long Trail crossing at Sherburne Pass marks the beginning of your hike. Follow US 4 east from Rutland or west

from Sherburne Center, to the height-of-land. The Long Trail Lodge is just west of the Long and Appalachian trail signs here. There is off-the-road parking on the south side of the highway. (This trip ends at VT 103 in East Clarendon. You'll have to make plans to return to your car from that point.)

Follow the white blazes south. Don't be fooled by the northward loop. The trail quickly begins a gradual, southerly climb between glacial boulders. After about 500 feet you reach a trail sign. It is 2.4 miles to the top of Pico from here. The grade becomes moderately steep as you swing sharply left. Stones fill the path, making the footing less certain.

The trail passes a variety of topographical features as it continues its steady climb. The path gouges into the earth before climbing over roots and ledge. Many spindly young trees fill the woodlands. You pass two huge glacial boulders, both supporting colonies of moss and several trees, on the left. After a looping S-turn, the trail widens and crosses damp, muddy areas.

Partridge thrive all through this section. It's exciting to hear their whirring wings and see the blurred shadows disappearing beyond thick branches. But

On the Long Trail

seeing the small, tufted head and wide, fan-shaped tail close-up is really breathtaking.

The climb from Sherburne Pass has led diagonally upward. At .6 mile the trail crests a low ridge, swings up to the left, and becomes more moderate. As it passes along the east side of the ridge, the pitch lessens still more.

Ferns dominate the forest floor, as you pass through yellow and white birches. The trail crosses to the west side of the ridgeline. Through scattered openings in the now-intermingling white birches and evergreens, you catch glimpses of Pico Peak ahead.

Sink Brook is on the right side at 1.1 miles. Swing left over ledge to the east side of the ridge again. Cut logs help you over a brook at 1.2 miles. Swinging right, the trail begins a long, steady climb. Evergreens predominate, as you walk through and beneath their spreading limbs.

At 1.8 miles you emerge onto a ski slope. Proceed upward along its left edge for about 500 feet to Pico Junction.

It is now .6 mile to the summit of Pico Peak via Pico Loop.

Continue straight up the ski slope for 100 feet and follow the blue blazes into the woods. The trail now gets very rough. It narrows between body-brushing branches. Twisting and turning, it courses up over rocks, roots, and ledge.

You cross three ski trails before passing beneath the Pico Chairlift. Ahead to the right is a wide, bare path leading to the summit. Microwave towers welcome you at the top. Primary views extend to the north and south. Killington Peak fills the area to the southwest.

On leaving the summit, retrace your previous route under the chairlift and bear right down the ski slope, keeping the ski patrol cabin on your right. Blue blazes will guide you through a line of trees on the right. Walk through them onto the road and down 50 feet to the blaze on the right.

A narrow, winding and sometimes steep descent over the next .4 mile brings you to Pico Camp. Built in 1959, this frame cabin has bunks for twelve people. From the clearing here you look south to Killington Peak and southeast to Mount Ascutney. This is the halfway point of today's hike and a good spot to rest awhile. A spring is located 100 feet to the north on the Long Trail.

Below to the right the Long Trail South begins a very long, gradual descent. For approximately 1 mile you hike along the west side of the ridge and enjoy the gradual ups and downs in the trail. One heavily rooted section offers the only change from the surprisingly comfortable going.

At 3.9 miles a steeper descent leads to a raised walkalong. Boggy areas lie ahead. Rocks and logs help you through them. You pass a .3-mile spur trail to Ram's Head Mountain on the left as the path returns to its level grade.

Killington looms ahead. At 4.3 miles a sign informs you that you are now halfway between Pico Camp and Cooper Lodge. You've only 1.5 miles left today.

The Long Trail recently has been relocated to the west side of Snowden Peak. Signs mark both ends of the change. No longer does the trail pass by the Snowden lifts. Enjoy the uninterrupted wilderness walking.

Your first noticeable climb since leaving Pico Camp begins at the northern end of the new route. The grade rises steeply over rivers of rocks and flattens out only occasionally along this revised section.

Approaching the Killington West Glade Ski Trail, the path swings right. Rocks and crusty roots make the footing wobbly. You cross several small brooks and walkalongs before reaching an iron pipe that drips spring water onto the trail at 5.7 miles.

The Juggernaut Trail joins from the left at 5.8 miles. Cooper Lodge is just ahead. This attractive shelter was constructed in 1939 by the Vermont Forest Service and extensively repaired in 1969

by the Vermont Department of Forests and Parks. The floor and most of the walls are stone. A picnic table, stove, and bunk space for twelve to sixteen people will make you comfortable tonight. Springs are located 100 feet south of the lodge.

Second Day

Cooper Lodge to Governor Clement Shelter

Class: III
Distance: 4.5 miles
Hiking time: 3 1/2 hours
Vertical rise: 610 feet

This day will include an ascent to Killington Peak. (The town that was once its namesake is today known as Sherburne.) A vast 360-degree view from Killington's summit is sure to impress you. Ascutney rises most prominently to the southeast. The White Mountains of New Hampshire are visible in the northeast. To the west are Mendon Peak, the City of Rutland, Lake Champlain, and the Adirondacks of New York State. You look down on the summit of Pico Peak to the north.

From Cooper Lodge take the Long Trail South. Folow its white blazes approximately 100 feet to a small clearing. Here the blue-blazed spur to Killington Peak leads east off the Long Trail. This .2-mile spur to the summit is a steep climb over jagged pieces of rock and ledge. Scrub growth edges the trail. Your first view of the top includes a lookout tower (not open to the public) and a radio installation. A spur to the east takes you to the Killington Gondola Terminal and Restaurant.

When ready to resume your backpacking journey, descend to the Long Trail via the Killington Peak spur and go left (south). The path follows an easy grade along the southwest slope. It is possible to maintain a smooth and

spirited stride over this undemanding
section of trail. Spruce and balsam spills
give the path its "bounciness."

You start an extended gradual descent .8 mile from the start of today's
hike. There's a quietness about this
evergreen-rimmed path. Kneel to examine the cloverlike clumps of wood sorrel. On an autumn morning their three-
part compound leaves may be delicately
outlined by frost. Chickadees abound.

Near a clump of wood sorrel there
may be a group of "creeping evergreens." Shining club moss is the
species that predominates here. Tiny,
bright-green, pointed leaves encircle its
erect stalks.

A gradual descent over a rocky path
leads you to the Tamarack Shelter spur
after 1.5 miles. A sign and the short
spur trail lead right to it. To the left the
blue-blazed Shrewsbury Trail goes
southeast toward Shrewsbury Peak. Continue on the white-blazed Long Trail. The
path maintains its gentle trend as it
crosses the east slope of Little Killington. At 1.8 miles you reach Consultation Point, elevation 3,750 feet.

After leaving Consultation Point, the
trail slices along the south slope of Little
Killington. It becomes narrower and very
rough as it winds around trees and over
roots and rocks. To the left, the hillside
slopes off steeply. Ever so slowly, you
make your way downhill.

After crossing two small streams, the
Long Trail swings sharply right at 2.6
miles. You have an easy, level walk
once again. Oak and beech are prominent in the deciduous forest to the sides
of the path.

Such open woods as these are the
blue jay's favored habitat. This handsome bird has an assortment of voices,
ranging from raucous calls to melodious
warbles. Blue jays include insects in
their summer diet, but they are primarily
vegetarians. Interestingly, they perform

an important reforestation service. By burying more acorns and beechnuts than they ever can eat, they help plant new trees.

About .5 mile from the last sharp turn, you cross a walkalong and turn sharply left onto an old road. Very quickly, you turn right off this road and continue on a path twisting through open woods.

Soon the trail crosses a road. It proceeds downward through more woods and emerges onto still another old road. It follows this one awhile before branching right onto a rocky, gutted path.

At 4.2 miles this trail descends some sturdy log stairs and joins a logging road. Follow it to the right. A rushing brook parallels the way on the left. Ahead you can see the roof of the Governor Clement Shelter. The trail winds left to a junction. A spur leads left to the brook and another swings right toward the stone shelter where you'll spend the night.

The William H. Field family of Mendon erected this shelter in 1929. It bears the name of Percival W. Clement, who governed Vermont from 1919 to 1921. Its deep-set bunks accommodate eight to ten persons. A picnic table and stone fireplace add luxury to the comfortable setting.

Third Day

Clement Shelter to VT 103

Class: III
Distance: 6.4 miles
Hiking time: 4 hours
Vertical rise: 790 feet

Two steep climbs to hilltops interrupt, and add diversity to, today's long, gradual descent. The walking is easy; you will have time to enjoy the surroundings.

From the shelter, descend to the road and turn right. Running water becomes audible on both sides. After .4 mile the left stream flows under a road bridge and joins with the stream on the right.

Another bridge appears at a wide bend in the road after .6 mile. Follow the white arrow into the evergreens just before the bridge. The flat trail dips down to the edge of the roaring stream. The steep hillside closes down to the path. Step carefully over the slippery roots along this very narrow part of the trail.

Yellow birches lead into thick evergreens as the path swings away from the water. Upper Road interrupts the tranquility at 1.2 miles—but only until you re-enter the woods on the other side.

The trail continues flat and narrow. It crosses several small brooks and many boggy areas. Few logs or walkalongs aid your travel in these muddy sections. Look to the sides of the trail for the firmest footing.

Much of the path is sandy as you continue within sound of the stream. The path winds along next to the water again. Such airy openness offers a nice change from the narrow, tree-lined trail. Rising steeply from the water's edge, the way leads over a hogback. It's a little like walking over a natural bridge. Streams rush by far below on both sides, as the straight path passes beneath towering evergreens.

The trail drops down to a dry brook bed and follows it to a junction with a wide stream. Pick your route and rock-hop across. Then switch back to the left and climb steeply up away from the stream.

You pass through more boggy areas before the Long Trail forks right at 2.7 miles. A mobile home and garage appear on the right. Keep left on the gravel road leading to the next mobile home on the left. Enter the woods again at the white arrow on the right and continue past yet another mobile home out onto Cold River (Lower) Road. Go right. Take the first left onto a gravel road and follow its uphill route. A white arrow (3.2 miles from Clement Shelter) guides you back into the woods to the right.

A long, steady climb brings you to the top of the ridge. You're likely to see golden-crowned kinglets anywhere along here. These tiny (three-to-five-inch) birds are a dull, olive-grey color, with golden crowns bordered by black and white. They can be seen feeding on branches of firs, spruces, or other conifers. Like the black-capped chickadee, they will often fly close to look you over.

The way descends from the ridge and passes over more boggy areas, before reaching the trail register and Hermit Spring at 4.3 miles. During dry seasons, though, water may not be available here.

Just after crossing the corner of a rocky pasture, the path winds through some unusual trees. These tamaracks (American larches) are northern conifers that shed their leaves in the fall. Short needles grow in tufts at the ends of abbreviated branches, giving the tree a spidery look. Tiny, scaly cones sit upright. Its tough root fibers were used by eastern Indians to bind birch bark canoe seams. Grouse, hares, red squirrels, porcupines and deer eat the seeds, needles, and inner bark.

The trail passes through the pasture again and crosses Lottery Road at 4.7 miles. It ascends steeply over rocks and smooth ledge to Beacon Hill. The elevation of this grassy knoll is 1,740 feet. Keep to the left of the signed telephone pole and begin the steep, winding descent.

The rocky descent culminates at Clarendon Shelter after 5.6 miles. The trail passes left of the shelter through the cleared area and swings right to a stone wall. Step over it onto the dirt road and go left. This flat road bears right at a fork and leads .8 mile to VT 103, where your backpacking trip terminates.

The Presidential Range: Lincoln Gap to Middlebury Gap

Time allowed: 3 days, 2 nights
Class: III & IV
Distance (one way): 17.7 miles
Hiking time: 13 hours
Vertical rise: 4,457 feet
USGS 7.5' Lincoln; USGS 7.5' Bread Loaf

Each of the eight mountains included in this north-to-south trip rises over 3,000 feet (the highest is 3,835 feet). From their summits and trails you'll see the New Haven River Basin with its semi-circle of towering peaks, the wide Champlain Valley, and a vast variety of mountains. Among this quiet splendor you'll bed down just above an isolated pond high on a mountainside. To enjoy all this to the fullest, make sure you've limbered up any rusty muscles well in advance.

This backpacking journey takes you over "Presidential Peaks" from the Lincoln-Warren Highway to VT 125. The U.S. Forest Service does an excellent job of maintaining the trails. They are free from windfalls and obstructions.

First Day

Lincoln Gap to Cooley Glen Shelter

Class: III
Distance: 4.6 miles
Hiking time: 3 1/2 hours
Vertical rise: 1,896 feet

The access road for this trip is the Lincoln-Warren Highway. Drive from either Lincoln or Warren to the height-of-

land. Ample off-the-road parking is available here. (You'll have to work out a way back to your car when the hike ends at VT 125.)

On the southern side of the highway, hike up the embankment. The slope steepens almost immediately. Lacking the switchbacks that will ease the later approach to Mount Grant, this first climb presents the most rugged vertical rise of the day.

The steeply sloping trailsides are forested with birches, beeches, and maples. At .6 mile you come to a flat-ledged area that offers limited views of southern peaks. Most prominent in the panorama before you is Mount Grant. To the west, you can look across Lake Champlain and see the Adirondacks in the distance.

Descend from this smooth open ledge into the woods. Occasional clusters of ferns fill the forest to either side. Infrequent sections of ledge and loose rock cross the packed-dirt trail. After the initial steep climb, you proceed more gently over small drops and rises and long, flat stretches.

As the path rambles through one such level section, it passes beneath a monstrous old birch tree. Twelve-to-fourteen feet in circumference, it leans its mass across the trail at a thirty-degree angle, resembling the elongated barrel of a great cannon.

Rougher footing marks a series of switchbacks. Farther on, cut logs provide traction as the path leads over level areas of black mud and across a ridge.

A small tumbling brook begins to parallel the trail. At 2.6 miles you cross it via two rough-hewn logs. The trail continues to wind its way upward along the west ridge of Mount Grant and shortly crosses to the east.

Picking your way over loose rocks and tangles of roots, you climb the steep east ridge. Intermittent views of near and far mountains appear through the trees. Needles carpet the way as the delicious aroma of spruce and balsam engulfs you.

After ascending areas of packed dirt and ledge sandwiched between shorter evergreens, you emerge onto level ledge: the summit of Mount Grant, elevation 3,623 feet. Signs direct you to the right for a close vista, which includes Mounts Cleveland, Roosevelt, and Wilson and Bread Loaf Mountain.

Beyond, to the south and southeast, are Killington Peak and Mount Ascutney.

It is .7 mile from here to the Cooley Glen Shelter. Your descent south from the summit begins steeply. It drops over long sections of smooth ledge and loose rock between stands of trail-hugging evergreens. Nimble stepping is needed around and down over these areas of ledge. Directly ahead Mount Cleveland comes into full view.

The trail becomes wetter as the grade lessens. At one point it veers sharply left around a particularly boggy area. Cut logs aid your passage over wet, muddy sections. Soon the path slopes more gradually and eventually becomes level. Packed dirt replaces the rocks and roots, making for easier walking. The way widens and continues through a great stand of fir and spruce to Cooley Glen Shelter.

This frame lean-to, erected in 1965 by the U.S. Forest Service, has room for six to eight people and will see you through your first night. Branching right from the Long Trail South just beyond the shelter, the Cooley Glen Trail leads 500 feet to a spring.

Massive birch over the Long Trail

Second Day

Cooley Glen Shelter to Skyline Lodge

Class: IV
Distance: 7.8 miles
Hiking time: 6 hours
Vertical rise: 1,966 feet

As you can see by checking the distance, today you will have a full day of hiking. Much of it is up and down an assortment of peaks. You'll want to be well rested and get an early start.

Leaving Cooley Glen Shelter, the Long Trail South climbs very steeply to the east. Twisting and turning, the path becomes moderate and even gradual as it passes through stands of balsam and spruce. The footing is rooted at times but rock-free. After a quick .5 mile, you arrive at the heavily wooded summit of Mount Cleveland, elevation 3,482 feet. No views.

Descend gradually along the east ridge. A short climb brings you across to the west side. Descending again, you pass through hundreds of handsome white birches interspersed with evergreens. This long descent offers occasional views of the other peaks you'll be visiting today. Stretching southward before you are Mounts Roosevelt and Wilson and Bread Loaf Mountain.

The contorted black skeletons of aged, dead trees dot the lower stretches of open woods. Their rough, shingled bulks rise imposingly among the younger surrounding trees. Shelves of mushrooms and fungi thrive on their surfaces.

The trail begins a moderate climb. It flattens out again, then rises gradually and begins a long traverse to the east. Becoming steeper, it swings right and returns to the west side of the ridgeline.

Crossing the ridge on a long, flat cut eastward, the path reaches the summit of Little Hans Peak at 2.1 miles. A wood sign gives the elevation as 3,400 feet.

Leading east from this summit, the path passes over occasional roots and a few rocks. Firs and spruces continue to perfume the air and spill needles on the trail.

At 2.4 miles from the beginning of the day's hiking, you cross a trickling brook and then climb easily to another long, wet, log-crossed area leading west. The trail winds back to the east and rises to a rocky overlook before crossing Mount Roosevelt's 3,528-foot summit. Descending in a southerly direction, Mount Wilson and Bread Loaf mountain are visible at close range straight ahead.

The path gradually climbs, then drops. Step carefully over ledge and loose rocks as you go steeply downward. At the bottom of this slope the Clark Brook Trail leads left to Granville.

The trail now begins a long ascent to Mount Wilson. You wonder at times where the peak is as the path descends over rocks and roots. Turning sharply left, the way scrambles moderately up over narrow ledge. Keeping to the east of the ridge, you make your way to the peak.

At the 4.8-mile point, you arrive at Mount Wilson, elevation 3,745 feet. The Long Trail leads to the right from this wooded summit. Before continuing, follow the short spur straight ahead for far-reaching views to the east and south.

Leaving Mount Wilson, the trail begins a short series of descents and ascents. It then starts a very long steep descent to Emily Proctor Shelter. Stepping down over precipitous sections of rocks and roots,you reach the shelter.

The Long Trail bears sharply left, crosses a brook, and passes upward over wet ground and rocks. At the 6.3-mile mark you enter a clearing containing a number of signs. The Long Trail makes a switchback left. Climb the right spur to the vista on Bread Loaf Mountain. You'll want to spend some time en-

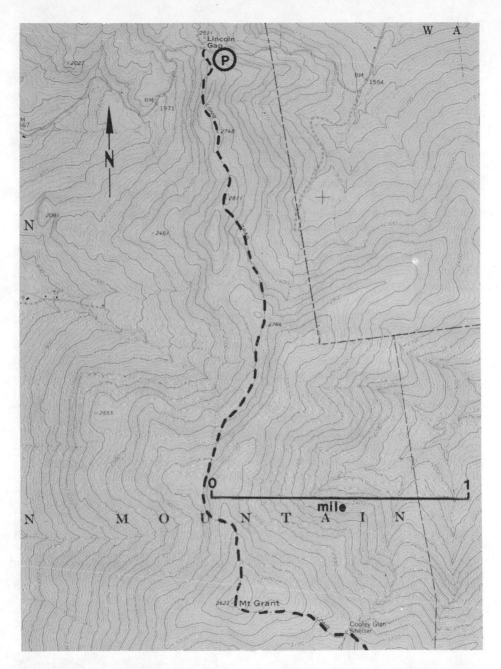

joying the expansive view across the Champlain Valley from this 3,835-foot vantage point.

Return to the clearing and proceed south. An interesting sign stops you after a short walk. Although probably not as meaningful to you as to a striving end-to-ender, it informs you that you are now at

the midpoint of the Long Trail—equidistant (130.4 miles) from the Massachusetts and Canadian borders.

Step down over a damp path. Long cut trees minimize the chances of sinking into the mud. Ledge marks the start of a very steep section.

Entering a clearing, the Skylight Pond Trail leads right toward Ripton. You are now only .2 mile from Skyline Lodge. Continue straight for roughly 100 feet and turn left at the sign to the Skylight Pond Shelter. Follow the blue blazes to the lodge and pond.

This picturesque spot rewards your long day's hike. The lodge sits on a bluff overlooking Skylight Pond. From its raised porch you look across the tree-enclosed pond to distant peaks. With bunk and loft space for ten, plus water at a nearby spring, you should be quite comfortable here.

Third Day

Skyline Lodge to Middlebury Gap

Class: III
Distance: 5.3 miles
Hiking time: 3 1/2 hours
Vertical rise: 575 feet

This last day of your backpacking trip offers an interesting assortment of hiking and visits to many overlooks. Climb up the steep trail behind Skyline Lodge to the brown-and-yellow sign directing you left to the Long Trail South. Go left and follow the white blazes.

At .2 mile on the Long Trail you pass over Battell Mountain. The elevation is 3,482 feet, but the heavily wooded summit does not provide any views. The gradual ups and downs of the trail frequently lead over boggy areas. Walkalongs aid your passage over these muddy sections.

After 1.2 miles your route passes a trail to the right for the Boyce Lookout. It leads 20 feet to a partial overlook to the west. A bit further, you cross over the wooded summit of 3,323 foot Mount Boyce. You know you are at the summit when you see a sign pointing the way back to Battell Mountain.

The Long Trail makes a fairly long, gradual descent, reaching Boyce Shelter after about 1 mile from the Boyce summit. It resumes behind the shelter and rises steadily, before leveling out and maintaining a rough route over the rocks, slippery ledge, and roots of the west slope of Kirby Peak.

The Burnt Hill Trail joins the Long Trail after another .7 mile. This path, maintained by the Middlebury College Mountain Club, leads 6 miles to Ripton. A brown and yellow sign to your left points out that Middlebury Gap is ahead. Continue on the white-blazed Long Trail South.

At the 3.2-mile point in today's hike, after a short ascent, you reach the rounded, ledged area called Burnt Hill. There is a partial view over tree tops to the west. Follow the trail as it leads sharply left off the hill.

The now-gradual trail makes a long descent through thin forest. In the process it crosses the ridge from west to east. Occasional climbs over gnarled roots onto ledged areas vary the hiking. You eventually enter a small clearing where an unmarked spur trail leads left to an eastern vista.

Back on the main trail, pick your way around more boggy areas beyond the clearing. After descending a long, moderate slope you come to a sign pointing left to the Silent Cliff Trail. From the cliff there are views to Monastery and Middlebury gaps.

The Long Trail swings sharply right from this intersection and makes a long, steep descent. After leveling out, it rambles briefly through the woods before emerging onto a small embankment above Robert Frost Memorial Drive (VT 125) at Middlebury Gap.

50

Mount Mansfield

Time allowed: 5 days, 4 nights
Class: IV & V
Distance (around loop): 17.1 miles
Hiking time: 18 hours
Vertical rise: 7,080 feet
USGS 7.5' Mount Mansfield

Much folklore has been woven around the origin of Mount Mansfield, Vermont's highest peak. One tale has it that a chap named Mansfield was pitched off Camel's Hump when the beast stumbled while kneeling to drink. He lies, stone-faced, staring at the sky and giving the mountain its famous profile. Another story claims that it Is the profile of Mishawaka, crippled son of an Indian chief, who perished on Mansfield's summit after crawling there to prove his courage and uphold his family's honor. Several stormy days followed his death, during which the mountain changed from one peak to the outline of Mishawaka's face.

There's a story about the naming of the mountain, too. The Abnaki Indians first christened it "Moze-o-de-be-Wado," meaning "Mountain-with-a-head-like-a moose." Its present name is derived from that of an English Chief Justice, Lord Mansfield, whose name also graced the town (now Stowe) that sits not far from the mountain's base.

The following backpacking trip will take you to most of the mountain's famous points of interest. All the sections of its distinctive profile are included: Adam's Apple, Chin, Lower Lip, Upper Lip, Nose, and Forehead. You will also visit the Lake of the Clouds, Bear Pond, Cantilever Rock, and Wampahoofus Rock.

Our route is chosen from the system of trails webbing Mount Mansfield. It includes the steepest half-mile of hiking trail in the state, as well as the highest point, the Chin, elevation 4,393 feet. Variety is provided by underpasses, switchbacks, crevices, caves, and ladder-and-cable climbing.

The mountain's trail system is maintained by the Green Mountain Club and the University of Vermont Outing Club. All the side trails are blazed in blue, while the Long Trail is blazed in white. The Green Mountain Club also cares for the Taft and Butler lodges, where you will spend your nights on the mountain. Nominal fees are charged for their use.

Mount Mansfield also has a Ranger-Naturalist in residence from May through November to help answer questions hikers might have. The rangers ask that while hiking above the treeline you stick to the blazed trails and walk only on the rocks. Mount Mansfield is one of only two arctic-alpine areas in Vermont. With increased use and accessibility this 250-acre area is being destroyed more quickly than it can regenerate itself. What appears to be grass around you is probably an arctic-alpine sedge and one of the seventeen endangered species growing on the mountain. Footsteps can easily destroy this fragile vegetation and leave the soil open to erosion, so *please* walk carefully and only on the paths.

First Day

Smugglers Notch to Taft Lodge

Class: V
Distance: 2.3 miles
Hiking time: 3 1/2 hours
Vertical rise: 1,920 feet

The Bear Pond Trail rises out of Smugglers Notch. Views to the peaks of the Sterling and Worcester ranges, the Lake of the Clouds, and Mount Mansfield's Adam's Apple and Chin await hikers who can meet this trail's challenge.

Make certain you are ready for this climb before starting out. Novice hikers have struggled up some of the steeper sections and reached the point where they could climb neither up nor down. Even experienced hikers find this trail a real challenge. The going is rugged and slippery in good weather and downright dangerous in bad. If you are conditioned and experienced, your climb up the steepest half-mile of hiking trail in Vermont will be exhilarating.

To arrive at your starting point drive north from Stowe on VT 108 past the Mansfield and Spruce Peak ski areas to Smugglers Notch. The blue-blazed Bear Pond Trail leads west from the road at the height-of-land. Watch for a yellow road sign saying "Steep Winding Hill" and the blue blazes just beyond. There is a parking area on the east side of VT 108 diagonally across from the start of the Bear Pond Trail. (You'll finish this backpacking trip at the Gondola Parking Area, just over 2 miles from your car.)

The trail climbs immediately up through clefts in small boulders, twisting over ledged areas. The gnarled roots of tenacious birches and spruce frequently provide the only footing as you scramble up these near-vertical slopes. Hands and feet search for these or any other supports in the cracked face of the ledge. If you are carrying a medium-to-heavy pack, remember to keep leaning inward to maintain your balance. A hiking stick can provide much-needed leverage. Watch carefully for the blue blazes.

The trail skirts an overhanging ledge. Winding around and mounting this ledge, you'll be rewarded by your first open view, east to the Sterling Range and down into Smugglers Notch. Climbing higher, you'll also be able to see the peaks of the Worcester Mountains to the southeast. An even more elevated look to the left lets you see the faded blue peaks of the White Mountains on the horizon.

Thick evergreens cling to the edges of the trail. A trickle of water flows slowly down, wetting the ledge and roots and turning the dirt path to reddish-brown mud. The going can be very slippery. A woodsman's cup helps you collect enough water to quench your thirst.

Although roping over the rocks is not necessary, there are many particularly smooth, steep sections. You will need to stretch and grasp your way cautiously. The numerous medium-sized rocks that litter the path do not always offer sure footing.

After this steep, steady climb of .5 mile to the ridge, the hiking becomes less arduous. There are even occasional flat areas. But here to greet you next are long series of black, muddy sections, alternating with still-steep rises in the trail. Logs can sometimes aid footing.

At .9 mile a short spur leads right to Bear Pond. This tiny mountain pond is well worth visiting. Its edges are surrounded by trees and rocks, giving it an aura of isolation.

Smugglers Cave o

Bear Pond

Bear Head

Smugglers Notch

P

Elephants
Head

BM ≈ 1803

Big Spring

Lake of the Clouds

APPROXIMATE BOUNDARY

M
A
N
S
F
I
E
L
D

Adams Apple

The Chin

BM 4393

Taft Lodge

THE

N

M O U N T

LONG

MANSFIELD

STATE

108

TRAIL

FORE

MOUNT

BDY

APPROX

BOUNDARY

Mount Mansfield Hotel

BM ≈
3849

The Nose

Ski Lift

APPROXIMATE

MANT

BOUNDARY

BM ≈ 3120

The Forehead

TOLL

ROAD

APPROX BDY

APPROXIMATE

BOUNDARY

0   1

mile

Butler
Lodge

MANSFIELD

Continuing, the main trail again opens to striking views to the east. It eventually winds its way to the Lake of the Clouds. This is the start of fragile alpine vegetation area. Walk carefully—and only on the path—to avoid disturbing the flora and fauna here.

After 1.8 miles the Bear Pond Trail ends at a four-way intersection. The Hell Brook Trail enters from the left and continues across to the right. Go straight, following the Adam's Apple Trail. It climbs steeply .1 mile to the top of Mount Mansfield's Adam's Apple. Elevation here is 4,060 feet. From the open summit enjoy a close view south to the Chin and a pleasant look down upon the Lake of the Clouds. Turn west for a look at Lake Champlain, stretching for miles in the distance.

Continue on the Adam's Apple Trail. It is marked by a procession of cairns and blue blazes as it descends another .1 mile to meet the Hell Brook and Long trails at Eagle Pass.

Follow the white blazes of the Long Trail North to the left. It slithers down over a spill of rocks paralleling a tiny stream. A hike of .3 mile brings you to Taft Lodge, a thick-logged cabin with bunk space for thirty-two, a toilet, which also serves as a composter, and ample water supply. You spend your first night here.

Second Day

Taft Lodge Loop

Class: V
Distance: 4.8 miles
Hiking time: 5 1/4 hours
Vertical rise: 2,973 feet

With a good night's rest behind you and a hearty breakfast under your belt, you are now ready for today's trails. You'll pass over very little level ground. The way is all up and down steep grades,

many of them wet and obstinate. Keep in mind, also, that most of the first half of the hike leads down, while the last portion is mostly straight up.

The Laura Cowles Trail, your route back to the Taft Lodge, is very difficult, especially after you have climbed the Chin and descended the Sunset Ridge Trail. It is steep, exceptionally rocky, and extremely wet. The going is a rugged, slippery, one-step-at-a-time process most of the way. Conserve your energy for it. By the time you return to Taft Lodge at the end of the day you'll have earned a nourishing meal and a full night's sleep.

We recommend this particular route only to those who feel they are in strong physical condition. A great deal of previous hiking experience is not necessary—but stamina is. You don't want the steep return climb up the western slope to become so punishing that you are too exhausted to continue. As long as you are returning to Taft Lodge for the night why not leave your pack for the day? You will enjoy this day hike much more, and it will make walking much easier.

From Taft Lodge walk back up the Long Trail for .3 mile to the intersection of the Long, Adam's Apple, and Hell Brook trails. (From here it is .3 mile to the summit of the Chin, and another .2 mile down to the junction with the Sunset Ridge Trail.) Go left onto the Long Trail South.

The way leads up over boulders and ledge. The path swings left around a sheer ledge face, up through a narrow crevice, and then intersects the Story Trail. The climbing becomes steeper as you look almost straight up toward your goal. Swinging around to the north end of the ridge you begin to realize how high you are. It is often possible to see a clear blue sky above you, rolling waves of clouds below.

Winding upward over lichen-covered

ledge, you soon come to the summit, identified by a U.S. Geological Survey marker. This is the highest point in the state—the top of Vermont. Take time to enjoy both the feeling of accomplishment and the views from this unparalleled vantage point.

On a clear day you can see farther than you'd have thought possible. Looking north and a bit east you can see the Sterling Range, Cold Hollow Mountain, Belvidere Mountain, Big Jay, and Jay Peak. If the view is clear, you can see Mount Royal in Montreal just west of north. To the northeast are the Lake Willoughby mountains, Bald and Pisgah. Swinging east, you can clearly see the Worcester Mountains backed by the Granite Mountains.

South of east is Mount Washington in New Hampshire. The Franconia and Kinsman ranges—also in New Hampshire— extend farther south. The Green Mountains as far as Killington Peak are seen to the south, with Camel's Hump especially prominent. Southwest, you see Whiteface Mountain. Stretching for miles along the western horizon is Lake Champlain and behind it, the Adirondacks.

Follow the blazes (white rectangles with red) across the bare summit and down to the open grassy area. Here you will find Profanity Junction. Look for the sign for Sunset Ridge Trail and State Park. You have now come .8 mile from the shelter. Go right onto the blue-blazed Sunset Ridge Trail. The path winds its way across the side of the ridge below the Chin. It passes over open ledge and down through scrub forest, eventually coming to the junction of the Story Trail. Stay on the Sunset Ridge Trail, go sharply left, and begin descending the open ridge on ledge and grass. Closely grouped cairns and blue blazes guide your way. Endless trickles of water wet the ledges.

As you crest a small knoll (well down the ridge), turn to see where you have been. The Chin rises commandingly above everything in sight. Trees increase in height as you descend from the scrub area and pass through leg-brushing balsam firs. The trail narrows and tunnels downward through these taller trees. Cresting a small knoll you are engulfed by hordes of skeleton trees and then surrounded by shorter green ones.

The path swings sharply left past a huge submarine-shaped boulder. From here to its distant junction with the Cantilever Rock Trail, the Sunset Ridge Trail descends like a bobsled-run over sheer ledge. It narrows, twists, and slithers, as trees close in along the sides. Views are limited to the path directly in front of you. Ledges are steep and smooth. Water slickens much of the way. Footing is often best along the sides of the path where you can hold onto trees as you pick your way down. Full concentration is a must.

At the 2.2-mile point you come to the Cantilever Rock Trail. Follow this .2 mile to the right. You will cross three brooks and many roots, and skirt several boulders, before coming to Cantilever Rock.

The seventy-five-ton rock is forty feet long and extends thirty-one feet without support beyond the cliff's edge. Sixty feet up in the air, it protrudes like the narrow prow of a sailing ship. At other angles it looks like a bowsprit of a square-rigged brigantine. A log ladder invites you to climb up for a closer look.

Returning to the Sunset Ridge Trail, bear right. It joins the Laura Cowles Trail .4 mile later. You cross several brooks via rocks and split log bridges. The trail becomes more gradual and extremely wet. Walk over a footbridge to the wooden bench. The Laura Cowles Trail begins here. Go left.

This trail is marked by blue blazes. It follows and crisscrosses a brook for quite a distance. It becomes progressively steeper as it climbs higher.

At 3.9 miles the way seems to stop at a high, horizontally ribbed ledge. Go right here if you have a pack. The path is extremely steep as it leads out over open ledge and intersects the Sunset Ridge Trail. Just ahead is Profanity Trail, which will lead you down a steep, rocky .5 mile back to Taft Lodge. This name might have been more appropriately applied to the Laura Cowles Trail, although it seems suitable here also.

Third Day

Taft Lodge to Butler Lodge

Class: IV
Distance: 4.2 miles
Hiking time: 4 1/2 hours
Vertical rise: 1,025 feet

As indicated by the lower vertical rise, today's exploration of Mount Mansfield will not be as taxing as yesterday's. However, the trails require the agility and physical conditioning necessary to maneuver through and over a succession of narrow ledges, steep canyons, and rocky tunnels. Bring along water; there will be very little until you near Butler Lodge, where you'll spend the night.

Hike back up the Profanity Trail from Taft Lodge, .5 mile to its junction with the Long Trail South. You will gain a rapid 600 feet of elevation in this distance. Go left onto the Long Trail South. Follow the white blazes with red rectangles across open ledge splashed with green map lichen. Stay on the marked trail to avoid damaging the fragile alpine vegetation.

The Long Trail cuts diagonally across the ridge to the west side and continues its southerly route. After hiking .7 mile from Taft Lodge you come to a sign for the Subway and Canyon North Extension trails. Go right onto the blue-blazed Canyon North Trail, which leads west from the Long Trail. After approximately 250 feet the Subway Trail enters from the right. The Canyon North Extension swings left here. Stay on it.

This soft, spongy path passes through thick stands of evergreens. These trees shelter you from the winds that often buffet the mountain's west face. Continue to follow the blue blazes as they lead steeply downward. The path rises to cross over big boulders and passes under an overhanging ledge.

After winding left, the Canyon North Extension forks. A spur branches left down through a cave. A gentler path circles around and over the cave to the right, joining shortly with the left branch. From the narrow ledge just beyond the southern end of this cave, there are excellent views (look back) of Sunset Ridge.

Occasional breaks in the trees alongside the trail offer intermittent views to the west across Lake Champlain to the Adirondack Mountains. After a bit of easy rock scrambling, the Canyon North Extension terminates at the Canyon North Trail 1.3 miles from the beginning of the day's hike.

The Canyon North Trail (also blue blazed) enters from the left at this junction and swings south along the west side of the mountain. Follow it south. Short, young trees hide the trail and make the footing uncertain. Soon a "windowed" cave is reached on the left. Blue blazes mark a steep ascent to the Long Trail above (but don't take it).

Squeeze yourself and your pack through the caves, crevices, and overhanging ledge. Watch carefully for the infrequent blue blazes. At one point you approach a long stretch of ledge rising vertically at the left side of the trail.

View to the Lake of the Clouds from Mount Mansfield's Chin

The path makes a sharp turn opposite a blue blaze near the beginning of the ledge.

You pass over an assortment of rocks, roots, and ledge, so the going is slow. The trail makes its only ascent, over loose rocks and small pieces of ledge, to its terminus (after 1.8 miles) at the blue-blazed Halfway House Trail.

Cross straight over the Halfway House Trail and continue south on the blue-blazed Canyon Trail. After a steep downward pitch the trail passes through a deep crevice. Rock walls rise high above. At the far end, a low rock tunnel leads into the canyon. You must remove your pack and slide it behind you as you enter through this low tunnel.

At its end, climb down the ladder to the canyon floor. The massive ledge walls lean outward to the right. Follow the trail as it tunnels down to still another level. It is again necessary to remove your pack and slither through the narrow opening.

The trail then emerges onto the mountain's western slope. There are more narrow passages between giant boulders before the path passes over open ledge offering fine views to the west. The Canyon Trail enters balsam and spruce woods and makes a steadily steepening ascent to the crest of the ridge. The Lake View Trail leads southwest on the right just before the Canyon and Long Trails intersect at the Summit Station.

Pause to enjoy a grand view of the eastern horizon. The nearby coin-operated public telescope will bring everything even closer. Snacks may be purchased here during the summer months.

Continue following the Long Trail South for .3 mile. It leads over a board-walk, through a wooded area, and onto the gravel road to the TV installation. Utilizing this road for a short distance, the trail bears right into the woods and

reaches the northern end of the Forehead Bypass just short of the TV station. Go left onto this white-blazed trail.

The Forehead Bypass begins a gentle descent over a soft dirt path. This ever-descending trail winds through open woods carpeted with a variety of green mosses. Cloverlike wood sorrel flourishes here, while clumps of ferns raise their delicate fronds above the lower greenery.

The South Link leads left off the trail at the 3.1-mile point of today's hike. Continue right on the Forehead Bypass. Increasing its downward slope, the way descends over smooth faced rocks. Roots traversing the path offer the only sure footing.

At the 4-mile point the Forehead Bypass reunites with the Long Trail. Go left onto the Long Trail and pass through the Needle's Eye. You then reach a clearing where a sign directs you left toward Taylor Lodge. Ignore this and look sharply right for the "Butler Lodge" sign. Follow this trail down to the lodge.

This structure was constructed in 1933 by the Long Trail Patrol. From its picturesque setting you may enjoy a panorama of views. Butler Lodge faces southwest down the chain of Green Mountains. To the west are the Champlain Valley and Adirondack Mountains.

There is good water in a small brook just east of the lodge. Bunks and loft space can accommodate up to twenty-four persons. This is a secure, cozy place to spend the night.

Fourth Day

You'll want to save this day as an extra in case of rain. If you are lucky enough to have five rain-free days, you might use it to explore some of Mount Mansfield's other trails. If so, we urge you to consult maps and descriptions of those trails before venturing out. The Green Mountain Club's Guide Book of the Long Trail would be a valuable help here. There is a section for just the side trails on Mount Mansfield.

Fifth Day

Butler Lodge to VT 108

Class: IV
Distance: 5.8 miles
Hiking time: 4 3/4 hours
Vertical rise: 1,162 feet

Today's route takes you to several new points of interest. You'll see the famous Wampahoofus. You'll also explore two final features of Mansfield's profile—the Forehead and Nose—and then enjoy far-reaching views to the east and southeast before making your final descent to the mountain's base.

The Wampahoofus Trail is exceptionally interesting. It begins at the right rear corner of Butler Lodge. The path leads north and eventually east for .8 mile to the junction with the Long Trail near the Forehead.

Almost immediately after leaving the lodge, the Wampahoofus swings sharply left. Your way is blocked by a vertical ledge you must scramble over. At .1 mile the Rock Garden Trail branches off to the left. Continue straight here. Balsams fill the woods and sweeten the air with their fragrance.

The Wampahoofus Trail leads steeply upward. It twists and turns constantly as it climbs over and around huge boulders. Circling under overhanging ledge, the path becomes wet at times. Step carefully, especially when climbing on wet ledge.

Stands of short, scrawny white birches edge the way as you climb toward massive outcroppings of ledge. The path seems to end abruptly at a

high ledge. Climb to the right side and enter the long cave leading upward through the boulders. Overhead a small window through the rocks allows sun to enter the dim interior.

Ahead is an endless variety of rock shapes. Keep a close watch for that petrified creature who roamed the area many years ago. If you have not spotted the elusive Wampahoofus by the time the Maple Ridge Trail intersects at .6 mile, go back about 50 feet and look up. He lies with open jaws, directly overhead to the left.

The Wampahoofus was orignally identified by Professor Roy O. Buchanan, founder of the Long Trail Patrol. According to Roy, the Sidehill Wampahoofus was a creature particularly well adapted to travel on Vermont's mountains. With legs shorter on one side than the other, it was adept at grazing and pursuing prey on the steep slopes. Unfortunately, due to extensive inbreeding all the females were born left-hand runners and all the males right hand runners. Thus, the males were unable to catch the females during mating season and no more Sidehill Wampahoofuses were born.

From the junction with the Maple Ridge Trail, the Wampahoofus turns sharply right and begins a steep ascent over smooth ledge. Natural indentations in the rock offer convenient footholds here. Scrub trees disappear, as the way continues steeply upward to intersect the Long Trail.

Continue on the Long Trail North .1 mile to the summit of the Forehead. A cairn-supported sign gives the elevation on this southernmost peak of Mount Mansfield as 3,940 feet. From here you can look out in all directions.

The Long Trail North continues through alternately rocky and black, muddy areas. Trees become taller and offer shelter from the wind, as the path dips slightly and begins a gentle descent to the TV road. Just before this junction the Forehead Bypass enters from the right.

You reach the TV road 1.2 miles from Butler Lodge. Go left down the road and pick up the Long Trail on the right. Walk up to the wooden platform and go up the stairs to the Triangle Trail and the Nose.

The elevation at the Nose is 4,062 feet. You can look back down upon the Forehead and up to the Lips, Chin, and Adam's Apple. There are views in all directions.

Blue blazes direct you eastward off the open ledge. The Triangle Trail extends .4 mile from the Nose to the Toll Road at the Octagon. It is a narrow trail that snakes over an endless succession of rock, ledge, and roots. Footing is slippery and at times precarious. Bushy balsam and spruce tug at your body as you wade through them.

The path leads to a small open lookout on the left. From here you have a spectacular view of the entire eastern side of Mount Mansfield—from the Chin to VT 108. Blue blazes continue to lead on a steep ragged descent.

Directly across the Toll Road you'll see the sign for the Hanson Trail. It begins by following the Nose Dive Ski Trail down very steep slopes. You might want to side step a bit, to relieve the pressure on your knees. Staying inside the high wooden fences, go straight, then right, then left, and finally right once again.

Just past the last fence, where the ski slope goes straight down, look diagonally across to your left for the trail's blue blazes on the trees. The Haselton Trail might aptly be called the "water way." You see, hear, or walk through water almost all the way to the bottom.

The path swings steeply away from the ski trail and passes through wet, rocky areas. It leads over a narrow ski trail, crossing and paralleling trickling brooks in the process. After .5 mile, it traverses a larger ski trail and enters the woods again on the other side.

You cross several smaller brooks before the trail rock-hops over the South Stream. Continuing downward, you suddenly find yourself remaining elevated while streams drop away on both sides.

This hogback becomes soft underfoot as it passes between rows of waist-high evergreens. Needles carpet the path as it proceeds straight and flat along the ridge. Taller firs with needleless limbs are passed before the younger, bushier ones take over again. By this time the streams have become faint rumbles far below.

Returning to its winding ways, the Haselton Trail begins a long, moderate-to-steep descent through thick woods. The path is soft and spongy underfoot. At the 3.3-mile point on this last day's hike it leads out onto a ski service road and follows it down to the Gondola Parking Area.

From here it is a short walk to VT 108 and a little over 2 miles back up to your car.

Guidebooks from
New Hampshire Publishing Company

Written for people of all ages and experience, these highly popular and carefully prepared books feature detailed trail directions, notes on points of interest, sketch maps, and photographs.

About Vermont—

25 Ski Tours in the Green Mountains, by Sally and Daniel Ford. $4.95
20 Bicycle Tours in Vermont, by John S. Freidin. $5.95
Canoe Camping Vermont and New Hampshire Rivers, by Roioli Schweiker. $4.95

For hikers—

Fifty Hikes in the White Mountains, by Daniel Doan. $7.95
Fifty Hikes in the Adirondacks, by Barbara McMartin. $8.95
Fifty More Hikes in New Hampshire, by Daniel Doan. $6.95
Fifty Hikes in Maine, by John Gibson. $6.95
Fifty More Hikes in Maine, by Cloe Catlett. $8.95
Fifty Hikes in Connecticut, by Gerry and Sue Hardy. $6.95
Fifty Hikes in Massachusetts, by Paul and Ruth Sadlier. $7.95
Fifty Hikes in Central Pennsylvania, by Tom Thwaites. $6.95

Other guides—

25 Walks in the Dartmouth-Lake Sunapee Region (NH), by Mary Kibling. $4.95
Discover the Adirondacks, 1, by Barbara McMartin. $6.95
Discover the Adirondacks, 2, by Barbara McMartin. $7.95
25 Ski Tours in the White Mountains, by Sally and Daniel Ford. $4.95
25 Ski Tours in the Adirondacks, by Almy and Anne Coggeshall. $5.95

Available from bookstores, sporting goods stores, or the publisher. For complete descriptions of these and other hiking, skiing, walking, canoeing, and bicycling guides for the Northeast, write to: New Hampshire Publishing Company, Box 70, Somersworth, NH 03878.